T0150769

TRUE FREEDOM

TRUE
FREEDOM

5 Choices to Help You
Overcome Your Obstacles
and Move Forward

Rick Bosch

NASHVILLE

NEW YORK • LONDON • MELBOURNE • VANCOUVER

TRUE FREEDOM
5 Choices to Help You Overcome
Your Obstacles and Move Forward

Published in New York, New York, by Morgan James Publishing. Morgan James is a trademark of Morgan James, LLC. www.MorganJamesPublishing.com

Scripture passages are taken from the Holy Bible, New Living Translation, copyright © 1996, 2004, 2015 by Tyndale House Foundation. Used by permission of Tyndale House Publishers, Inc., Carol Stream, Illinois 60188. All rights reserved.

ISBN 978-1-64279-936-1 paperback
ISBN 978-1-64279-937-8 eBook
ISBN 978-1-64279-938-5 workbook
Library of Congress Control Number: 2019919227

Cover Design by:
Rachel Lopez
www.r2cdesign.com

Morgan James is a proud partner of Habitat for Humanity Peninsula and Greater Williamsburg. Partners in building since 2006.

Get involved today! Visit
www.MorganJamesBuilds.com

TABLE OF CONTENTS

FOREWORD
by Stephen Arterburn

Along the way, in our fallen world, outside the garden of Eden, we struggle, and we eventually get stuck. We want freedom from our habits or obsessions or wounds or addictions. We seek help and often hear perhaps the most misquoted, out of context, scripture. It comes from John 8:31,32 when people only state the phrase, "the truth will set you free." If that were true, all we would need to do is memorize scripture and we would be free. It does not work that way because the phrase, "the truth will set you free", in context does not promise freedom simply by scripture memorization or picking a particular verse to apply to a particular problem. There is much more to finding freedom. The entirety of this passage says that if you will follow the teachings of Christ, you will become a disciple of Christ. Being a disciple of Christ, by following the teachings of Christ, is what allows you to know the truth and then the truth will set you free.

The problem comes when our humanity gets in the way of following Christ. We try and fail. Then we try harder and fail harder. Some repeat this hopeless process over and over again, and nothing changes. It's called true insanity. This is why "True Freedom" is such an important book. It begins where transformation begins. Not with futile effort to create change under your own limited power, but with surrender to God who is all powerful. That is just the first of the many choices the book guides you through. Follow the directions here and by the end you will be free.

By picking up this book you have already made a great choice and taken a huge step toward true freedom. Get the support you need to stay the course. Remember that awareness of a problem is better than denial but it does not change anything. Desire for change is better than satisfaction with living in a self-constructed prison. Awareness and desire must be accompanied by willingness. Not just a one-time statement of willingness, but a daily, humble, death to self-will and surrender to God's will. Daily surrender to the path found here in "True Freedom" will lead you to be truly free.

INTRODUCTION

Every person has a beginning. George Washington's life began in colonial Virginia; Winston Churchill's in Woodstock, England; Elvis' life started in a place called Tupelo Mississippi; and mine…well, it started in Hazel Dell, a small town right outside of Vancouver, Washington. Perhaps you may be thinking, *I know where Vancouver is.*

Let me assure you that it's not by Canada or in Canada. I lived most of my life explaining to others that Vancouver is in Southwest Washington right across the river from Portland, Oregon. Most people know where Portland is, and they know it as the place of constant rainfall. And, yes, there is a lot of truth in that belief; Portland can also be a very beautiful place because of the rain.

The population of Hazel Dell at the time I was born was only 691. Of course, the town with its one main road didn't seem that small to me because I didn't know any better. Stores were sprinkled on each side of the road for a couple of miles. The townspeople had everything that they needed—schools, parks, a Fred Meyer grocery store, Smokey's Pizza, and a Burgerville. Burgerville was the place to get the best burgers in town. When you don't have much, much isn't expected. For me, Hazel Dell was the place where my journey began.

I lived in a normal house with a normal family, believing my life was normal. I would later discover that *normal* was not as normal as I had thought. I was not blessed with any brothers and had only one sister who was three-and-a-half-years older than me, which made life challenging during our childhood.

When I was in elementary school, she was promoted to junior high, i.e., seventh through ninth grade in the 1970s. When I went into seventh grade, she moved into high school. When I finally made it to high school, my sister had just graduated.

Because of our three-year age difference, it made it difficult to build a close relationship. During those growing-up years, we ended up taking two different paths. I was the shy child who never got into much trouble (or never got caught), and she was…well, let's just say that she was different than me.

Thankfully, however, I did feel that we really bonded a few times. One day some friends of mine and my sister were playing baseball in the street. I hit the ball, and my sister retrieved it as I was approaching second base. She tagged me, and I immediately declared in no uncertain terms, "I was safe!"

"You were out!" she stated forcefully.

We began arguing and screaming at each other while the other players looked on. With no umpire to solve the dispute, my sister decided to enlighten me. She grabbed me, threw me into a nearby mailbox, and I headed home with a broken arm. I spent several years in therapy trying to deal with what happened. I'm just kidding!

While I was growing up, both of my parents worked outside the home. My dad was a maintenance supervisor for a manufacturing company, and he also worked a second job at a local gas station on weekends. In those days when a customer pulled into the gas station, an attendant pumped the gas. He additionally checked the oil, washed the windows, and checked the air in the tires—all for free. Back then, the price of gas was peaking at twenty-five cents a gallon. What happened to those days?

My mom, who loved to bake, worked as a baker at our high school. Her schedule was perfect. She started early in the morning and was off by 2:00 when we arrived home from school. I still remember my Mom baking fresh bread and cinnamon rolls every morning at the school. A slice of bread sold for five cents and a cinnamon roll cost twenty-five cents. I didn't have to pay anything because I knew the *right* people, namely Mom. When I was in high school, my mom would always have a piece of warm bread with butter waiting for me when I walked into the school cafeteria. Let me be honest, it's all that I had, but that slice of bread started my day in a positive way. I still dream of that soft bread and butter melting in my mouth with each bite.

The years of my youth seemed to go by so quickly; in fact, they seemed to pass by like a blur. I will share a few memorable moments throughout the book. When I graduated from high school, my life would change in a huge way. I still remember sitting with my classmates in the gymnasium, where an empty seat couldn't be found. The temperature was high, and we waited impatiently for the speeches to finish.

When I finally walked up and received my diploma, I returned to my seat to wait and wait…and wait some more. My last name starts with a "B," so you can imagine the wait with over 400 seniors in my graduating class. When the last name was finally called, we all tossed our caps into the air and celebrated our accomplishment.

What happened next was one of life's defining moments for me. On my drive home, I began to think about my future, and I felt this uncertainty inside of me. I had closed one chapter in my life, but I didn't know how to start the next. For the past year, I had been working at a retail store, but I hadn't formulated any solid plans beyond that. After I went home, I felt depressed, so I decided to go and see what my friends who had graduated with me were doing.

I found out that many of them had gathered at a place by the Columbia River called Frenchman's Bar. This was a sandy park area near the river. When I arrived, I found most of them were partying hard and celebrating their "freedom." I guess they thought that this was the place where true freedom could be found. I parked my truck and began to wind my way through the maze of my classmates drinking, smoking, and having sex. I felt entirely out of place and a deeper sense of loneliness came over me. Nothing felt right to me, and I felt like I didn't belong. A part of me was saying, "Join in and have fun," but another part was telling me to leave, so I left.

One of our greatest desires is freedom, which we value, pursue, and want to experience. Our country is built on freedom. Our constitution lists specific freedoms, including the freedom of speech, the freedom of the press, and the freedom of religion, which have become the fabric of our nation. For me, when I finally felt free to do anything that I wanted to do, to go anywhere I wanted to go, and to become whoever I chose to be, I felt lost. What happened?

Why did the freedom that everyone looked forward to in high school feel so distant to me? Could it be that I didn't understand the meaning of true freedom?

Having freedom doesn't automatically bring satisfaction; in fact, freedom can actually place us in bondage. A dictionary definition of *freedom* is "the power or right to act, speak, or think as one wants without hindrance or restraint." When we consider freedom in that regard, this intangible sounds so good, doesn't it? When you really think about "doing something without any hindrance or restraint," you realize we have all sorts of freedoms, and with that freedom comes consequences.

Let me share an example: You can say whatever you want to whomever you want, but that other person may not like it and retaliate with some of his or her own freedoms either in words or actions. When I was 17 years old, I began complaining about my job and how things were being managed.

One day the general manager called me into his office and said, "I heard that you don't like what you are doing and how things are being done around here. It's up to you. You can either quit complaining and do your job or find another job."

I learned very quickly that indeed, I had the freedom to choose. Did that freedom feel good? Not really. I was free to complain, but the consequences were unemployment. I decided to shut my mouth and submit to my boss. Guess what? I ended up outlasting him in the company.

The lesson that I learned that day was that freedom always has consequences. When we have freedom, and we make a bad choice, we will find ourselves suffering in pain. Suffering is what happens with addiction. Freedom allows us to choose to drink or use drugs or gamble or eat because all can bring a sense of satisfaction—at first. The longer we continue making these unwise choices, the more entrapped we become. The very freedom that we desired to have becomes the very thing that has taken that freedom away from us.

Over the last 15 years, I have been a pastor working with people with all kinds of struggles in their lives, including addiction, loss, anger, relationship issues, and abuse. My desire has always been to assist others in finding help, hope, and healing in their lives. The pages of this book contain many of the principles that I have learned throughout my lifetime. No matter what you are facing, let me assure you that there is hope. How can I say that? Because I have seen it happen time and time again over the years—not only in others—but it my own life.

I want you to begin by looking at the following list and circling the degree to which you struggle with each area of bondage. Be honest as you evaluate your life.

Symptom/Behavior	Degree of Struggle
Alcohol	1 2 3 4 5
Anger	1 2 3 4 5
Anxiety/Fear	1 2 3 4 5
Control Issues	1 2 3 4 5
Drugs	1 2 3 4 5
Food/Overeating	1 2 3 4 5
Gambling	1 2 3 4 5
Internet Over-use	1 2 3 4 5
Lying	1 2 3 4 5
Overworking/workaholic	1 2 3 4 5
Pornography/Sexual Purity	1 2 3 4 5
Prescription Drugs	1 2 3 4 5
Rebellion	1 2 3 4 5
Shopping	1 2 3 4 5
Smoking	1 2 3 4 5
Stealing	1 2 3 4 5
Video Games	1 2 3 4 5

If you were to choose one area from which you want to be free, which would it be? This book was written to help you find freedom from that area.

Someone has said that the choices that we make, make us. In the following chapters, you will learn the importance of making five choices, each of which is essential in leading you toward freedom. Next, you will learn about taking several actions that support each of those choices. Think about this: every day we make thousands of choices, most of which we don't even consider. But what if we were able to make specific choices that could change our lives for the better? What if those choices could lead us to freedom? Would it be worth it to you? I hope that as you read the following pages, you would consider making each choice and see where it will lead you.

A profound verse in the Bible is found in John 8:32, which says, *"And you will know the truth, and the truth will set you free."* This book invites you to know truth, and I believe that this truth will lead you to freedom.

Do you want to experience true freedom? Keep reading…

Chapter 1
THE CHOICE
OF SURRENDER

S unday, September 2, 1945, one of the most significant days in history, was the day that Japan signed the surrender and ended World War II. The resulting casualties in this bloody war numbered in an excess of 50 million lives. The formal surrender happened on the *USS Missouri,* a battleship that saw significant action in the Pacific Ocean. Surrender did not come easy. This decision was highly debated decision between Japan's supreme war council. Some did not want to surrender but fight until the very end; however, Japanese Emperor Hirohito convinced the board to take the step of surrender.

When General Yoshijiro Umezu signed for the Japanese armed forces, his aides wept as he wrote his signature. Can you imagine what these leaders were feeling inside? I am sure that the feeling of failure and disappointment was overwhelming. Many wars have been fought throughout history, but one fact is true when it comes to battle: you fight to win. What you don't do, is surrender.

Something in all of us rejects surrender. Surrender is accepting defeat, and no one is excited about that decision. I played football, basketball, tennis, and track when I was younger, and my goal was to win. The problem with that goal is that you don't win every time, and when you don't win, you are faced with the reality of losing. How you handle loss will be a test of your character, and admitting defeat surely became a test for me.

The late Evangelist Billy Graham said, "When wealth is lost, nothing is lost; when health is lost, something is lost; when character is lost, all is lost." Character is the qualities that make you the person that you are; things like compassion, patience, self-control, and honesty. Losing tests your character but losing can also grow and stretch your character. I have found that growing and stretching commonly happens through the most challenging tests of life.

When I was 19 years old, I was like most teenage boys; I was looking for a girl. One Friday night, two of my friends and I decided to go to the skating rink. Yes, I did say skating rink. Where else would you go to pick up some girls in Hazel Dell, Washington? As we were skating around the track, trying to impress others with our skills, a beautiful girl caught my eye. As I began to plot how I could get her attention and ultimately meet her, a thought popped into my mind; my opportunity would come when they announced the couples' skate.

A few minutes passed, the lights dimmed, the music changed, and I heard the announcement for which I had waited: it was time for the couple's skate. I rolled over to her and asked, "Would you like to skate with me?"

"Sure," she replied.

I couldn't believe my ears! My heart was pounding as she held my hand, and we started skating, talking awkwardly at first, and exchanging names.

The very next thing she said was a question. "Are you a Christian?"

I was somewhat taken aback but also relieved and answered, "Yes."

She then told me that if I wasn't a Christian, she was not interested."

I felt relieved. We talked for the rest of the evening and exchanged telephone numbers. From that day on, we began to date exclusively, and we talked every chance we had. A year and a half later we were married, and we lived happily ever after—not! At the time, I believed that everything about married life would be fantastic. But I quickly learned when you put two imperfect, broken people together who are entirely different in every way, something will go wrong, and it did. Both of us were very stubborn, and we didn't know the meaning of surrender. I was expecting her to meet my needs, and she was expecting me to meet hers.

Our verbal fights escalated until sometimes we did not speak to each other for days. Why would I allow that lack of communication to permeate our home? Well, I had watched my parents behave in precisely the same way. Hurt people hurt people. The only emotion that I knew how to express was anger.

Many tend to think that anger is represented by yelling and screaming, which can be true, but anger can also be conveyed by total, resounding silence. Anger that is turned inward punishes others with complete silence, and I resorted to this form of anger all too often. Every time I became angry, I felt terrible—like a failure. I told myself multiple times that I would not get angry the next time, but nothing changed about the way I expressed myself. No matter how hard I tried, I continued to hurt Kathy and later our children.

What I needed to do was surrender and admit that I needed help. Can you relate to my situation? Perhaps your struggle involves food or pornography or alcohol or video games or, like me, even anger. You tell yourself that you need to change, but you find yourself caught in the same vicious cycle. Our marriage was built on unresolved conflict, which only serves to build walls—not bridges.

After two and a half years of being married, Kathy became pregnant, which was quite a shock to us because we weren't really trying. At this time in our relationship, things were not going well. We seemed to be fighting often and nothing was really changing. The way that we handled our conflict was to avoid it and try to move on. "Time heals all wounds" or at least that's what I often heard while growing up. Kathy and I looked good on the outside, but inwardly, our life was in a turmoil, literally crumbling.

Shortly before Christmas, we were blessed with a beautiful baby girl we named Chrystal. We quickly learned that a baby means many things change, and they surely did for us. Chrystal was a colickly baby, crying for hours from the pain caused by gas or blockage. Her colickly nature continued for several months, exhausting Kathy physically and emotionally. I was of little help with the care of the baby, which caused our relationship to drift further and further apart.

My focus was on work and volunteering at our church. Kathy was also working at a hair salon part-time and then coming home and taking care of Chrystal. We seemed like we were the average family, but the insecurity inside of both of us caused even more turmoil.

When couples refuse to seek help or don't know how to find help, something is bound to go wrong, which is precisely what happened to us. That critical stage was finally reached when I discovered that Kathy was becoming emotionally involved with another man. Ironically, the person was one of our best friends.

I remember the day that I found out what was happening, I was shocked, I felt like my life was falling apart. I also had this feeling deep inside of me that said, "I was responsible". I knew that I had neglected her needs, and I had emotionally pushed her away. After admitting our failures to each other, we were able to work through our struggles; however, we never went to a counselor or took any steps to really address the deep wounds that were still there. We simply pushed ahead—like always, without confronting the real issues.

After another year went by, we tried to have another child, thinking the addition of another baby would help solve our problems. Unfortunately, we were unable to get pregnant so we decided to go to a fertility doctor, and after a couple of years of testing and treating, Kathy gave birth to another girl named Shannon. Soon after her birth, Kathy was pregnant again, and our third daughter arrived we named her Heather.

Do you see a pattern? I don't know what the doctor did, but all of a sudden, having children wasn't a problem. Our house was full with Kathy and I and the three girls. The next problem that arose between us was my desire for a son, but Kathy was done with having children. Could anyone blame her? After pleading with her multiple times,

I somehow convinced her to agree and try one more time for a boy.

The day we learned that Kathy was expecting, we were so happy but a bit fearful. No matter whether she was carrying a boy or a girl, we would love that child the same. We both knew that this child would be our last. The next several weeks were filled with anticipation. We decided that we would wait to learn the baby's gender when he or she was born. On December 30, that day finally came.

We rushed to the hospital in Portland, but her usual delivery did not go as we had expected. As the baby was being delivered, the umbilical cord got pinched, and the oxygen level plummeted. Suddenly, nurses and doctors flooded into the room. Everything was happening around me too quickly for me to process. I stepped away from Kathy's bedside—not knowing what to do, feeling totally helpless. Images of what could be, flashed through my mind.

Within a short time, Kathy was rushed into the operating room for an emergency Caesarean-section. My heart was pounding, and I was praying that God would protect the baby and Kathy. As I stood by her head, the doctor delivered the baby and finished the procedure. Both the baby and Kathy were fine. We welcomed Justin Dean into the world; after a long wait, our first son had finally arrived. He had a big smile, blonde hair, blue eyes, and weighed over nine pounds at birth.

To us, Justin was perfect in every way. When we took him home, we felt so blessed to have him join our family, which was finally complete with three girls and a son.

On the day before May 4, 1993, Kathy took Justin to the doctor for his immunizations. When she got home, he was a bit fussy and not feeling well. As we wrapped up our day, she put him in bed for the night. As always, I would wake up early for work and the first thing that I would do is to check on Justin and the girls. As I walked into his room, I knew immediately that something was wrong; he wasn't moving. I felt as if I had one of those moments when time seemed to stand still. My heart sank as I wondered, *am I having a bad dream?* I grabbed him, only to find that he wasn't breathing at all.

"Kathy! Kathy, come quick!" I screamed. As she came running from our bedroom, I told her that Justin wasn't breathing and she began to panic.

We could have called "911," but we only lived a half a mile from the hospital, so I grabbed the car keys and took Justin into my arms and drove as quickly as I could to the hospital. As I ran into the emergency room with him in my arms, one of the nurses on duty recognized me from church. "Rick, what's wrong?" Even as she listened to my quick account, I could read the look in her eyes that said without saying, *It's not good.*

She grabbed Justin from my arms and rushed him into one of the rooms where a team started to work on him. Kathy soon arrived, and within minutes, many of our friends from church came to offer their support, praying for a miracle. The nurse who had taken Justin came and told us the news that no parent ever wants to hear: Justin was gone.

The most difficult tests in life will test our character, and our family was now in the trial of our lives. We learned there are no guarantees in life. We go through our routines each day without really thinking about what is at stake. Losing a child brings a definite realignment of what matters.

- You see people and situations differently.
- You evaluate your life, your family, and even your future.
- You also ask questions about everything like:
  - Why would God finally give us a son and then take him from us?
  - Is God punishing us?
  - Is losing our son a test of our faith?
  - Did we do something wrong?
  - Could we have done something to prevent this?

So many questions ran through our minds. The deep loss that we experienced would forever change us.

I started this chapter talking about surrender. It was on May 4th that I personally surrendered. Surrender doesn't mean that we give up, but we do wave the white flag. It means that things need to change. We view surrender in terms of winning or losing but it is much deeper than that. Surrender is recognizing that we are no longer in control nor do we have to be.

Many tears were shed from losing Justin. I cried so hard that I didn't think that I could possibly shed one more tear. We were both emotionally exhausted. When we wondered how we could possibly move on, the answer came through our friends, who brought us food, visited us, checked on us, and prayed diligently for us. We felt as if they were standing in the gap for us.

A few weeks after we laid Justin to rest, I remember praying with Kathy for another son. We knew the possibility was slim, but we had to ask. Ours was a prayer of surrender, knowing that we were not in control. As the summer was ending and school was only a few days away, Kathy told me that she was expecting. You can imagine that we were thinking, *the odds were stacked against us*.

After several weeks, we decided to determine the gender of our child. As we went to the appointment, my heart pounded in anticipation. I was unable to think about anything else. I have to be honest; if Kathy hadn't been carrying a boy, I would have been a bit disappointed.

The nurse put the gel on Kathy's stomach and started the ultrasound. I looked at the monitor and had no idea how she could tell the baby's gender, I couldn't tell one end from the other! When the nurse asked, "Do you want to know?" we both answered "Yes!" in unison.

"It's a boy!"

We both felt a flood of emotions as we heard those three words. We were so excited and so thankful.

On April 13, Kathy went into labor. We rushed to the hospital, and her delivery again presented a challenge. I felt like I was living a déjà-vu experience. When the attending team broke her water, the baby's head again rested against the umbilical cord. The room full of nurses and doctors rushed Kathy to the operating room. *Was this really happening again?* My heart was pounding, and of course, my worst fears flooded in my mind. *Are we going to lose another baby?* I watched as the surgeon performed the emergency C-section, and within minutes, the nurses held our healthy baby boy, Jacob Dean.

When I was growing up, I had watched actors like Clint Eastwood, Harrison Ford, Mel Gibson, and Tommy Lee Jones act the part of tough guys who never backed down. However, I had to learn that surrender was much different than acting tough and not backing down. Real toughness is admitting our weaknesses and our need for help. Contrasting the two would only be the beginning of my understanding or need for surrender.

I always thought that I was normal but what I thought was normal was much different. Normal means being ordinary or average or typical. I thought that ordinary people don't have a lot of issues. That's why so many of us try to mask or hide our problems. We are trying to be normal or just trying to fit in. We fear that if others find out what I am really like then they won't accept me. But that is not what normal means. Normal means a person that reveals or shows others that they do have issues, that they are not perfect. When we learn to be normal like this, we get our first taste of freedom.

There seems to be a value system that determines how bad or good people are. I have to wonder who created this value system that somehow exists. There are certain issues such as drug addiction, sexual addiction, and abuse that are at the top of this list, while things like lying, excessive video gaming, overeating, or overspending are move acceptable.

The Bible offers a much different view of this value system. Romans 3:23 says that everyone has sinned and fallen short of God's standard. The word *sin,* which is actually an archery term, means "to miss the mark." When an archer shoots an arrow and misses the bull's-eye, he has "missed the mark."

When we don't follow all that God has told us to do, we "miss the mark," or we sin. I don't know about you, but I know that I sin every day. If you are anything like me, then we are both a couple of sinners. God has no value system or hierarchy because He doesn't see anyone differently; in God's eyes, we are all the same.

Learning this principle changed my life and my thinking. I didn't feel ashamed or of less value than others. No! I realized that I was a sinner—like everyone else. But what do we do about these issues or struggles or addictions we face?

Often, we try to overcome them by our own strength or willpower, but our tenacity or toughness or self-disciple only lasts temporarily. The Latin meaning for the word *addiction* is "to give over to" or "surrender." We give ourselves over to or surrender to drugs, alcohol, sex, gambling, anger, food, spending, work, exercise, and even our cell phones. The end result is that all these avenues end up controlling us. We try to stop, but there is something inside of us that drives us to continue, which is exactly what I experienced with anger. I didn't want to say one more word, but I couldn't hold myself back.

When I lost our son, it broke me, and I reached the end of myself. Up to that point, I tried to control everything in my life, but I didn't do a very good job. I had hurt my wife, my children and I couldn't even protect my son from dying. This was my moment of surrender. Surrender is our choice. If we do not surrender, then we will continue to do the same things over and over again because we are still trying to be in control. I have tried this path, and it does not end well.

The reason why I wrote this book is to help us learn that making different choices can truly set us free. Because surrender is the first choice that we must make, I want to address the actions that we need to take to surrender.

Action 1—Doing Whatever It Takes

For many years I knew that I needed to change, yet I didn't take the initiative. Knowing that I needed to change and actually doing something about it were light years apart. Actions speak louder than words, but the right actions are critical to real change. We must ask ourselves this question: am I willing to do whatever it takes to change? If we are not, then the likelihood of having lasting change are very slim. I hope that you are willing.

Certain things can prevent us from changing. They act as a wall or barrier between where we are and where we want to be. Let me share a few of them with you.

Apathy

The first wall, which is called apathy, doesn't mean "I don't care about changing"; it simply means, "I don't care enough to change." Albert Einstein said, "The world won't be destroyed by those who do evil, but by those who watch them without doing anything." You can know that you need to change, you can see that your situation is causing pain, you can even tell others about your problem or struggle, and yet you do nothing. The whole scenario seems kind of crazy, but it happens all too often.

How many marriages become roommates? The couple knows that they have problems, but neither one is willing to do anything to initiate change. They drift further and further apart—spiritually, physically, emotionally, and mentally.

How about working a job that has become increasingly mundane with no challenge to the point of simply putting in your time for a paycheck? Each day is more miserable, and though you hate your job, you do nothing about it.

When I was struggling with anger, I knew that I needed to change, but I didn't do anything about seeking help. I believed that I could change the emotion through my own willpower over time. Mine is a fairly common belief: if I ignore it or wait long enough, then it will get better. All I would say is good luck. I have tried that line of thinking for many years, and nothing changed. I have met person after person who has also tried this line of thinking and again, nothing changed. The cure for apathy is caring enough to do something. Let me ask you: do you care enough about your life to do something? My hope is that you do.

Pride

The next wall that inhibits change is pride, which says, "I don't have a problem" or "I can handle matters on my own." Pride erroneously believes:

- "I am better than others."
- "I am different than others."
- "I don't need any help; I can do it on my own."

I can identify with pride because I have been prideful throughout my life. I have fallen prey to the type of thinking that says, "I am not like everyone else. I don't really have that big of an issue. I will work harder, and this won't affect me anymore."

On August 31, 1986, two ships collided in the Black Sea off the coast of Russia. Of the 1,234 people on board the cruise ship, the *SS Admiral Nakhimov,* 423 perished as they were hurled into the icy waters. It only took seven minutes after contact to sink the ship. An investigation revealed the cause of the accident had nothing to do with the two ships, rather by human error. For nearly eight miles, the captains of the two ships had been aware of each other's presence. Both could have steered clear, but according to news reports findings, neither captain wanted to change course. Each was too proud to yield first. By the time the two men came to their senses, it was too late.

This illustration reveals exactly what pride does. We refuse to change until it's too late; sadly, before we come to our senses, we end up hurting many people. The book of James, which is one of the most practical books in the entire Bible, gives us instructions on what to do and what not to do. The purpose is to bring benefit to our lives—not pain. James 4:6 says that God is opposed to the proud, but He gives grace to the humble. This is important advice for us all. Imagine momentarily that God is opposed to you—not just neutral or apathetic—but actively against you. Knowing that He is battling to break you is not an encouraging thought.

Why would God oppose the proud? Simple! When we are proud, we are saying, "I don't need God! I can handle the situation on my own. I am more capable than God at solving a problem or repairing a relationship or healing pain." In a nutshell, we are saying, "I don't need You, God. I've got this."

On the other side is humility, which says, "I know I can't handle this situation or repair this relationship or heal my pain. I need Your help, God; I can't do this on my own."

James 4:6 concludes by saying that God gives grace to the humble. *Grace* is "receiving something that we can't earn, and we don't deserve." Grace is hard for us to understand or receive. Humility starts when we can admit that we need to change, and we ask God for help. He tells us that when we do, He will be there with His grace to do what we cannot do. We choose pride or humility with each decision we make. Pride will tell you that you don't need to change; humility will tell you that change is your greatest need.

Fear

One more deterrent that keeps us from changing is fear. The fear I am addressing is not the fear of spiders or snakes or the fear of heights or small places. This fear is far more deadly! Have you ever seen a marriage falling apart or a family member locked up in addiction? Why doesn't someone decide to change?

I personally believe that fear keeps them from changing. Fear paralyzes us, keeping us stationary, convincing us that if we attempt to do something, we will get hurt. This fear comes in many forms—the fear of failure, rejection, abandonment, loneliness, and even death. If you were to choose the fear that most affects you, which would it be? Recognizing our fears is important because they change how we think and what we do or don't do.

I have had to come to grips with a couple of my own fears. The first would be the fear of failure, which started when I was a young boy because I never felt like I was good enough. When I was in school, I wasn't the smartest, the most athletic, or the most talented. Receiving anything less than an "A" in a class brought feelings of insignificance, incompetence, and inadequacy. These same feelings also overwhelmed me when I played sports. My parents started me a year early in school, so I was always one of the smallest kids in my class. When I was in eighth grade, I tried out for football. I worked hard, impressing the coaches, but I wasn't big enough for my position, so I was assigned to the junior varsity team.

As an older teen, I joined a church basketball league. Each week we would play a different team in our city. When I didn't play well, and our team lost the game, I would be up most of the night, replaying the game in my mind, focusing on my mistakes and how I should have played better. If you hadn't guessed already, I had issues.

Even as an adult, when I started speaking in the church, I would continually evaluate my talk, especially if I felt I had forgotten a point or misspoke. If I perceived that my talk didn't seem to connect with people, I felt like I had failed. Each time that feeling of failure occurred the further it reinforced that belief in my mind: I am not good enough, and I don't measure up to others.

Failure is closely associated with pain, it attacks our self-worth. If I fail, I feel like I am less than others. If I don't perform to a certain standard, I feel less acceptable to others. Fear can also prevent us from taking risks. If I do and fail, then I will face additional pain, so why take the risk? People who play it safe are often those who have a fear of failure.

I also struggled with the fear of rejection. When I was a child in grade school, a group of kids constantly picked on me. When sides were chosen for games or activities, I was always the one who was consistently left out or ignored.

This is rejection at the core. My natural response was to stay away from those kids, and I did.

When I was in the eighth grade, I thought a certain girl was really pretty. Every time I passed her in the hallway, my heart would start beating, and my hands would start sweating. I would imagine asking her to the school dance, and we would have the best night ever. The problem was, she didn't even know who I was. This wasn't good. I knew I needed to introduce myself to her, but fear stopped me from doing it. As the date for the dance approached, I finally worked up the nerve to ask her to go, and she said "No." To say I was devastated would have been an understatement.

Being rejected affects how we relate to others. We can be afraid to get too close to others because of the possibility of being rejected. Fear of rejection keeps us from engaging emotionally with people; consequently, we settle for only surface relationships. People who battle feelings of rejection believe "If I get too close to someone, that person will eventually reject me." Rejection translates to pain, which keeps us from getting too close to others.

When I was 16 years old, I worked in a donut shop, and my job was handling the front counter. People would come in, browse at the many donut selections, and then place an order. Assembling their order and taking their money was simple and straightforward. Within a couple of months, the owner approached me to ask if I would become one of the supervisors, which meant more responsibility and closing up the store for a whopping ten cents more an hour.

I was only 16 years old, so what did I really know about managing? One day the owner noticed that the coffee machine wasn't clean, so she fired me—no talking, no warning—a done deal. The firing was both failure and rejection combined. These types of raw experiences can manifest into trust issues. No wonder fear can influence what we do and don't do. Each one—apathy, pride, or fear—can prevent us from moving forward.

A powerful motivator for us to change is a simple word called *pain*. Who wants to continually deal with pain? Nobody! I happen to believe that pain is a gift. Pain sends us a message that says, "Something is wrong," and that message will not go away until we do something about it.

One day a woman came into our building, needing to talk to someone. I was available, so I introduced myself to her and asked, "How can I help?" She started becoming quite emotional, and tears began streaming down her face. I gave her time to compose herself, and she shared about being molested as a child. "I am now in my early sixties, and this pain that is still deep inside of me keeps resurfacing."

We can try to cover up pain, or we can try to dismiss our pain, but ignoring it doesn't take away the pain. What had brought her to the place of seeking help? She finally came to a place of saying, "I don't want to push the pain down any longer; I need the pain to go away." Pain is like a sliver in our foot that continues to bother us until we remove the object.

Have you reached the point of saying, "I don't want to hurt anymore?" If so, you are at an excellent place to start because beginning to change will be determined by what we do or by what we don't do. My friend, are you willing to do whatever it takes to change?

Action 2—Identify the Consequences

I was wearing shorts, a t-shirt and some flip-flops. Life was good. I pulled the lawnmower out of my shed, checked the gas, yanked the cord, started the engine, and I began cutting around the outside edge of my large rectangular yard. Then I proceeded to walk back and forth, back and forth to cut the remainder of the lawn. As I cut, I enjoyed the smell of freshly cut grass, which I love. Everything seemed to be going as it had so many times before when all of a sudden, I heard a loud bang, instant pain stabbed through my foot. I fell to my knees in agony. I looked at my foot to see pieces of metal stuck in my skin, and blood was flowing everywhere.

Instantly I tried to stand up but the pain was too much. I yelled for Kathy, and she came running to our back deck. My next-door neighbor heard the commotion, looked over the fence, and instantly realized I had sustained a severe injury to my foot. He and one of his friends rushed over, helped carry me to our car, and we raced to the hospital.

As I sat in the emergency room, I wondered, "What went wrong? How did this happen?"

Hours seemed to pass before the nurse called my name. After I was taken to an examining room, a doctor came in to look at my foot. "What happened?"

When I told him that I was mowing the grass, he scolded me for wearing flip-flops. I didn't know that I was going to get in trouble with the doctor.

Apparently, a metal clothes hanger had been left in our yard by one of our kids, and when the mower blades hit the hanger, pieces of shredded metal were expelled like a gunshot. The x-rays revealed three pieces of metal lodged in the bones of my foot. That injury was the most painful experience I had ever felt. I learned a valuable lesson that day; our decisions will always have consequences. On that beautiful summer day, I had decided not to go into the house and put my shoes on. It was easier to wear my flip flops and mow the grass. I also decided that I didn't need to check my yard before mowing. My decisions cost me dearly with a trip to the hospital, surgery, excruciating pain, and rehab for several weeks.

Whatever we choose to do in life will have consequences—either favorable or unfavorable. As you look at the behavior or addiction that you want to be free from, it's important, to be honest with yourself. There can be good things that you receive from it like comfort, security or even pleasure. But with the good can also come the bad. Comfort can bring pain or shame afterward. The security that we feel can actually cause insecurity later on. And the pleasure that we pursue can fade away and leave us searching for something else. Let me explain what I mean by using an illustration.

A good friend of mine became addicted to pain medication. Like many people, he had back issues, and upon seeking a doctor's help, opiates were prescribed. Of course, the meds worked well and brought the desired comfort, allowing him to do his work. But with each day that came and passed, he began needing more and more of the drug. When the doctor finally cut him off, he was in full-blown addiction and went to the streets to find what he needed. He tried to hide his habit by lying to his wife, but his secret was eventually revealed. Their finances had been drained, and the trust between his wife, who felt betrayed, and him was shattered, straining their relationship.

My friend faced many consequences from his struggle with addiction. If we fail to list those consequences, we do not realize the full effect of our actions, which is essential to know in the healing process.

I want to share about my struggle with anger because I know its damaging effects firsthand. My anger affected my marriage in a multitude of ways. Anger was a weapon that I used to control, and that weapon robbed my wife of the love she deserved from me. My anger ripped us apart and affected our intimacy. The words that I used or the silence that I chose caused my wife great pain. My anger caused my kids to fear me and to pull away from me at times.

Anger affects all of our relationships because we become unpredictable in our words and actions. When I was working for a company, I was responsible for all of the drivers and their deliveries. When one of my drivers forgot to pick up an important delivery from one of our stores, I received a phone call about the problem that he had caused. The worse part of it was that I yelled at him in front of several other employees after he returned. Afterward, he came to me almost in tears, and said, "If you ever treat me like that again, I will have to quit." Some supervisors would say, "Great! Go ahead and leave." Deep down inside of myself, I knew that I was wrong. This lack of self-control only serves to push others away from us.

Briefly, I want to share some of the negative effects that result from unrestrained anger. Anger can have significant consequences on our health, causing headaches, migraines, stomach issues, high blood pressure, chest pains, depression, anxiety, and even cardiovascular problems. Another unfavorable consequence that I experienced was its negative affect on my self-worth. I had thought that I could handle my anger issues on my own, but when my willpower didn't work, I felt like a failure. Anger may feel good at the moment, but we later recognize what we have done and should have done. Just like any other drug or destructive behavior, we then find that anger gives us what we never wanted. Instead of boosting a person's self-worth, anger tears it down.

This action step is not designed to make us feel guilty or shameful; rather to help us take an honest look at the results of our actions so that we can ultimately change them. When we ignore or move away from them, we stay in our rut. When you look back at the particular behavior or addiction that you chose in the introduction, how has it affected your relationships? Your job? Your marriage? How about your health? And then it's always important to look at how it's changed you. That bondage may have seemed to be your friend—the one that you knew so well—but what has it robbed you of or of what is it robbing you?

Taking an honest look at the consequences helps us understand how much we need freedom. Let me ask you an important question: whatever area you need to work on, what would your life look like without it?

Action 3—Finding Help

I love to travel and explore new places. I have been known to go to a new city and just start driving with no idea of where I am going or where I am at. My love of exploring new places can genuinely drive my wife crazy! My one of many weaknesses is refusing to stop and ask for directions. I don't know why it's so hard for me to stop and ask, but I have found that many men have a similar problem. I think that our inability comes down to something called pride. Something inside of me says, "Don't do it! You don't need any help." I believe that I will eventually figure it out on my own. And, yes, sometimes I do find what I am looking for, but other times, though I hate to admit it, I am completely lost!

When it comes to making significant changes, we must come to the place of recognizing that we cannot fix ourselves and that we need to find help outside of ourselves. As I have already mentioned, pride will prevent us from making necessary actions that need to be made. My entire life was built on trying to fix myself or fix the problem.

"I can do it."

"I don't need any help."

"I will work harder."

Have you ever made any of those statements? They are some of our go-to answers. We eventually say, "This time it will be different because this time I am really going to try."

Some studies have indicated that people can change their behavior for 30 to 45 days before returning to the same old behavior. Whatever the number is, the objective isn't trying to stop something for a short period of time; it's changing something for good.

Realizing that I cannot fix myself comes from the understanding that if I could fix myself, then I would have fixed myself. The definition of *insanity* is "continuing to do the same thing, expecting different results." Some of us are insane because we keep doing the same thing repeatedly, trying harder and harder without seeing any change. We literally end up back where we started.

As a pastor, I meet many people who have loved ones with all kinds of issues. They contact me to ask if I would call their loved one and talk to them about their problem. I always ask, "Do they want to change?" Then I follow up their answer with the question, "If they want to change, then you need to have them call me." My answer sounds somewhat harsh, doesn't it? But what I have found is that if the person doesn't admit that he has a problem, and if he doesn't want to change, then the person is wasting his time and my time.

In our church, I lead a program with many groups designed to help others with their struggles. Often, I have people who want to buy the book and go over it themselves. I try to discourage them because, in essence, they are relying on their own strength. What happens is that they end up missing out on the support and encouragement that comes from others. The market for self-help books is 800 million dollars per year, and that number grows each year by 6 percent. The total self-help industry nets more than 10 billion dollars, which includes personal coaches, audio books, seminars, motivational speakers, apps, and other products. People believe that they can make the needed changes themselves. Why else would they spend that kind of money?

I have learned that if we fall into the belief that the answer is found in our working harder, we will not have sustained change. Believe me, I have tried working harder time and time again, gaining absolutely no ground. In fact, I will tell you what depending on myself did give to me: discouragement and hopelessness.

If you have realized that you cannot fix yourself on your own, then the next step contains your answer. Imagine the freedom that comes when we acknowledge that we don't need to fix ourselves. The pressure is off! I personally believe that it's perfectly acceptable not to be okay. The answer is found in seeking help outside of ourselves, but we must seek the right source of help.

Action 4—Surrender to Christ

Surrender says, "I can't do it myself; I need help." When I graduated from high school, my life was really going nowhere. I didn't have direction, I didn't feel good about myself, and I literally felt depressed. At the time I was working full-time at a warehouse with a couple of other guys. I became good friends with one of them whose name was Jay. We started to hang out together, and we discussed all kinds of subjects from politics to sports to religion.

One day as we were loading a truck, Jay asked me "Rick, would you like to go to church with me on Sunday?"

I wasn't at all prepared to hear that question. I didn't want to go to church, and I had no intention of going to church. I couldn't stand church and attending a church service would be the last place where I would ever spend my time. Before I even had a chance to formulate a response, the word "Sure!" came out of my mouth. *What am I doing?* my mind screamed at me. I knew I needed to come up with an excuse. I mean, I didn't know what to wear or how to act or what I was walking into. The work week finally ended, and I only had a day to figure out what I was going to do.

When Sunday arrived, I reluctantly decided to go ahead and go. I guess I didn't have a choice since he was picking me up that morning. I remember our driving up to the building and walking through the doors of the small weathered-looking building that looked like it had been built 50 years earlier. I saw wooden pews lined up in rows with an aisle down the middle. Probably less than a hundred people were sitting there, and as we walked in, they all seemed to be looking at us. The men were wearing suits and ties, and the women were all in dresses. We had to be the youngest people in that room.

I felt completely out of my element, and all I could think about was leaving. After listening to a couple of songs that I didn't know or understand, the pastor stepped up to the front and started talking. He opened the Bible and started to read from it. Even though I was completely uncomfortable, something he said resonated in my heart. He asked, "If you were to die today, would you know for sure where you would spend eternity?" I knew the answer: "No."

As a matter of fact, that question had been running through my mind for a couple of years. I kept thinking about the purpose of life. *Why am I here? What will happen when I die?* Not knowing the answer to these questions was a big reason for my insecurity. The pastor's words continued to run through my mind all week. I decided to go back to that little church week after week. Something was stirring deep inside of me, but I didn't know what it was.

One Sunday in May, I went to church with Jay and another friend as usual, but this day was different. After the pastor had shared, he asked those who had never surrendered their lives to Jesus Christ to come forward. I was literally shaking as I sat in that pew. I knew that I needed to make that choice, but I was so scared. I remember silently saying to myself, if someone else goes forward then so will I. I waited which seemed like forever and then I saw a few others stand and made their way to the front of the room, this was my chance. I stood and walked forward to the pastor. He talked to us about the decision that we were making and then prayed. On that day, my entire life changed. I would have never guessed that by surrendering, my life would begin to take a different course, but it did.

I am sharing my story because I have seen literally thousands of people make that same decision as I did and with it came positive change. When we recognize that we can't fix ourselves, then we must surrender to someone who can. We can listen to a plethora of good people in the world, but none are capable of what God can do when we are talking about freedom. Let me briefly share with you what surrendering to God looks like.

First, we admit that we aren't perfect, which is fairly easy. If we were perfect, then we wouldn't need help. The Bible calls this sin, which means, "missing the mark." When we do not live the way that God tells us to live, the Bible calls it sin. *"For everyone has sinned; we all fall short of God's glorious standard"* (Romans 3:23). The key word in this verse is *all*. The fact that we are all in the same place reinforces the fact that none of us are good enough. So, if we fall short, then how can we have eternal life?

Let me share one more verse: *"For the wages of sin is death, but the free gift of God is eternal life through Christ Jesus our Lord"* (Romans 6:23). A wage is something that we earn. Those who work a job understand wages. The Bible says the wages of sin is death. What we earn from sin ("missing the mark" or not measuring up to God's standard) is death. The payment for sin sounds very hopeless, but the good news is the free gift of God is eternal life! Jesus came to this earth and lived a sinless life. He was arrested and put to death on a cross to pay for our sins. Jesus paid the price for our disobedience, our selfishness, and our pride.

Because of what Jesus did, He offers us a free gift. It wasn't free to Jesus because it cost Him His life. We can't earn this gift; we have to accept it or receive it. The way that we do this is simple. We admit that we have fallen short in life, that we have disobeyed God. Then by faith, we believe that Jesus came to the earth, He was arrested, crucified and died. Most importantly, Jesus didn't stay in that grave; He rose again after three days. Since we were not there to witness it for ourselves, it is a step of faith.

Faith is believing in something that we cannot see. The Bible says that without faith, it's impossible to please God. I am not suggesting that a person just blindly believe. Do your homework. If you want to study further about the historical facts of Jesus' life, then I would suggest reading Josh McDowell's book, *Evidence that Demands a Verdict: Life-Changing Truth for a Skeptical World.* Lastly, we need to allow God to take control of our life. When I took this step, I prayed the following prayer:

> *Dear God,*
>
> *I need You. I know that I have disobeyed You. By faith, I believe, Jesus, that You came to this earth and died for me and that You raised from the dead. I ask*

*You to come into my life, to forgive my sins, and to
take control of my life from this day forward.*

If you have never taken this step of surrender or if you
are unsure of where you will spend eternity, then go ahead
and pray this prayer right now.

The importance of surrendering to Christ is that we do
not have to move forward alone. We have Christ to help us
do what we cannot do ourselves.

Action 5—Surrender Daily

We cannot control many things in life—the weather,
the traffic, politics, the economy, or what people are going
to do or say or what they feel. In truth, there really are very
few things that we can control. Surrender is about willingly
giving up control.

What I have personally found is that the only way we
will willingly give up control is if we trust. If I know that
you love and care about me, then I will find it easy to trust
you. But if I have questions about your character and I
don't have a history with you, then trust is not something
readily given. As we get to know God better, we learn that
He is trustworthy. He never changes and is always available.
When we understand who God is, then surrendering to
Him each day becomes easy.

When I was younger, my view of God was wrong. I
had picked up bits and pieces of opinions throughout my

formative years that were simply not true. I heard that God is sitting on His throne looking down at me. If I broke one of His rules, He was ready to bring judgment on me. If I made a mistake, then God would punish me. This kind of thinking made me fear God. I also believed that God really didn't care about my life. After all, He had too many other things to worry about. You can see how believing false facts about God will affect how you relate to Him. Why would I want to trust a God like that? My wrong view of God only made me pull away from Him. In contrast, having the right view of God is critical when it comes to surrendering.

A few years ago, I was working for a church in Vancouver, Washington, where I had been for fourteen years. We helped start the church with four other families, and we had seen incredible growth. But as time marched on, things began to change. Both Kathy and I had a feeling that God was preparing us for something different, but we didn't know what it was. This can be a difficult place to be. The days and weeks marched on and still nothing happened.

One day I received a message from someone I had met at a conference the previous year. He told me that his church was starting a recovery group, and they were looking for someone to lead it. "If you know of anyone, would you please let me know?"

As I stared at the message, I began to think about his question. I went home, told my wife, and we both agreed that I should contact him and ask some questions. This man worked at a church in Albuquerque, New Mexico, and I had to look at a map of the country to find out where it was. I had never even been to New Mexico. Both of our families lived in Washington, which would mean a drastic change. If this opportunity worked out, we would be moving away from our friends and family, including three of our daughters. This is where surrender comes into the picture.

We began to pray about the opportunity, and we decided that if God opened the door, then we would go wherever He wanted us to go. I am not naturally a person who likes change or is given to change. I worked for a company for over 25 years. I was a part of starting two churches, and I was with each of them for 14 years. What in the world was I thinking?

Well, one door opened after another, and we accepted the position in Albuquerque. A change was about to become real. Now let's talk about surrender. We had one of the most challenging decisions waiting for us. The only house that we had ever known was the one that we lived in Washington. As we continued to add to our family, we had added to our home—three different times. In fact, the house doubled in size from the time we purchased it. We knew that we needed to sell the house, which seemed simple enough—if it wasn't for the fact that the economy and the housing market was in terrible shape. This sale would not be easy. We talked to a couple from our church who were real-estate agents, and so we listed our house with them.

Meanwhile, I had to move to Albuquerque to start my new adventure. Two of our children were still in school, so my wife stayed in Washington until the house sold. We planned to move her and the kids to New Mexico when school ended, which was two more months. The days and weeks moved on, and we had a total of zero showings on our house. We believed that God was in control, and we were sure that He was sending us to Albuquerque, but there was no movement. I talked to our real-estate friends, and they told us that our house was *unique*. I am not sure that *unique* is good when it comes to selling. They said that out of 100 potential buyers, only one or two would be interested in a house like ours. Weren't we the lucky ones!

We were down to our last week before the kids finished school, and we didn't have a single offer. We had dropped the price twice in the six weeks the house had been listed. We had reached panic time! I remember falling to my knees and praying, "God, I know you opened up the door for us to go to New Mexico, and I know that there were no guarantees. So if we were to lose the house, then I know that you will take care of us."

I knew I had to surrender the whole matter of the house selling to Him, which was not easy. The next day I received a call from my former church in Washington, and the receptionist told me that a man who was moving from another part of the state was looking to buy a house. She had informed him about my house and wanted to give me his information. She gave me his number, and I immediately called him. After talking and exchanging information, he asked me my rock-bottom price for the house.

Normally this negotiating would have been handled by the real-estate agents, but I went ahead and told him. He was very interested and said he would come and look at the house. That weekend he and his wife traveled to Vancouver, looked at our home, and made an offer that same day which we accepted. If that all sounds unbelievable, here's the really astonishing part of the story: I flew to Washington and loaded all of our belongings in a moving truck. The next morning as we were pulling out of our driveway to head south, the new owner pulled up to our house with his truck to unload!

Throughout those two and a half months of changes, we had to learn how to surrender each day. We had to know and believe that God was in control. The temptation to take back control was always prevalent, but every time we did, we only experienced stress and anxiety. No matter what you are facing—alcohol, pills, porn, anger, or something else, daily surrendering is critical. We don't have to live life on our own. We have God to help us through each battle we face. Freedom comes when we admit that we don't need to be in control. Always remember that nothing takes God by surprise. Nothing is beyond His help.

My challenge to you is surrender to God each day when you awaken. Tell Him that you need help, that you need to change, and that you cannot do it on your own. Then as you walk throughout your day, keep depending on Him and see what happens.

Chapter 2
THE CHOICE
OF OWNERSHIP

When Kathy and I were first married, we found a duplex apartment to rent. We were so excited to be in our own place, starting our new life together. The apartment, which had two bedrooms, one bathroom, a large living area, and a kitchen, was all we needed moving forward. However, after living there for a few months, we soon discovered a couple of challenges. The parking was less than adequate, and we had no garage.

I had grown up in a home that always had a garage, and the garage was my dad's domain. He loved to work on cars and owned about every tool known to man. Let me re-phrase that: he had multiple pairs of every tool known to man. The only problem that he often faced was finding what he needed because he had so many tools. I knew that I needed a garage. Not that I knew how to work on cars, but I did like to work on projects. Well, after a couple of years of paying rent, we were ready to purchase our very first house. We only had one problem: no down payment. Have you ever been there before? You want something, but you don't have the money that you need?

During this time, my wife was working at a hair salon. One of her clients was a real-estate agent, so she shared our dilemma with her. Wouldn't you know that she and her husband were also experts at creative financing? I had no idea what creative financing meant, but I later learned that it means getting into a house without having any money. That was us! Creative financing was a perfect fit.

A week later, the real-estate agent took us to see a house they owned and were willing to sell on contract. We were excited. We signed the contract and moved in within a couple of weeks. Two years later, the couple approached us again about purchasing the house, even dropping the price of the place ten thousand dollars if we would cash them out. Within a couple of days, we went to the bank and were approved for a loan. We became homeowners. Have you ever wondered why we say that we are homeowners when the bank usually owns our home? An interesting fact is that only 29 percent of people own their home free and clear. We were obviously not in that group, so we started our thirty-year journey of paying a monthly mortgage; however, ours would last much longer.

Ownership comes with many benefits—building equity, tax deductions and having the freedom to do what you want to do with your property. But with the benefits comes a cost, including challenges like repairs and maintenance. When we were living in the duplex, we didn't have a yard, so we had no upkeep. Our new house had a huge yard, and the previous owners had planted trees and bushes everywhere. And when I say *everywhere*, I mean everywhere—with absolutely no rhyme or reason to their plan as well as failing to remember that plants and trees will grow! The driveway and the front of the house were bordered with large juniper bushes. I tried digging one out with a shovel, and I think my neighbor felt sorry for me, so he offered his pickup and chain to use. I humbled myself and welcomed his offer. My neighbor, my dad, and I pulled each bush out by their roots, and my yard suddenly looked twice as big. Now I was faced with a huge mess of bushes in my driveway.

Since I worked at a warehouse with delivery trucks, I decided to bring home a 26-foot-long truck. We filled it up from one end to the other with the juniper bushes. Oh, did I fail to mention that I am allergic to junipers? When the needles touch my skin, I break out in a rash. Imagine what I looked like after I loaded that truck.

The previous owners had also decided to plant four maple trees in the backyard. I feel relatively sure they looked nice 20 years before, but they had also grown to the point of ruining our roof and the roots were starting to break our patio. Funny how you don't see these issues when you are considering purchasing a house.

One day Kathy was helping me with lawn work, and somewhere she came into contact with some poison ivy. Her entire body broke out in hives. She was expecting our first daughter at the time, and the resulting rash and blisters made that summer most miserable for her.

These memories of ownership represent only a few of our challenges, but we also enjoyed many positive memories as well. What is true is that ownership can be demanding at times.

Our life is similar. We can do whatever we want, but the result will be positive or negative consequences. We are responsible for the decisions and the choices that we make. How do some people lose a job while others are promoted? Why do some marriages end within the first two years while other couples are happily married for decades? Why do certain people go to jail and others never get a speeding ticket? I have known several people through the years who have made bad choices and yet never own them. They continue to use excuses and bend the truth. Living this kind of life will not end well, and it will stop us from living free.

What you do and say matters. When we are young, we tend not to think much about our actions. We feel like we can do whatever we want and seldom think about the consequence, that is until something happens like an accident or an overdose or a divorce to give us a wake-up call. Life is short, and chances are, we will face different challenges and uncertainties.

The second choice is taking ownership. It is owning what we have done in the past and accepting where we are today. Taking ownership doesn't mean that we have to like what we have done or where we are, but owning it is so important. The following are the action steps of ownership.

Action 1—Take Responsibility

When we take responsibility for the choices that we have made, then we can begin to move forward. Unfortunately, we learn how to be a victim, or we use other tools that shift responsibility on to someone or something else. Not taking responsibility for our choices can seem to benefit us for a time. We can get away with lying or stealing or gossiping about someone, but eventually, our actions will catch up to us. This kind of thinking keeps us stagnant and unable to experience freedom.

When I was working in a warehouse years ago, I used a forklift to move pallets of fertilizer from one area to another. If you are not familiar with a forklift, they are machines with four wheels, and they have two forks on the front that slides under a pallet so that you can move or stack the product. I became very proficient at moving pallets and operating the forklift. However, if you are not paying attention and the forks are not in the proper position, you can slice into the product, which happened to me on several occasions. I justified the damaged bags in my mind, thinking, *it's all part of the job*. Imagine what it looks like to have a trail of fertilizer following you behind the forklift. That was me.

When my boss would ask, "What happened?" I would fabricate some story about the bags being broken when they were delivered to us.

What I was doing was avoiding or not taking responsibility for my actions. Why do we fail to own our mistakes? Most of the time we are trying to escape punishment, but I do believe making excuses goes far beyond that thinking, reinforcing how we feel about ourselves. I did not receive much encouragement from my father when I was growing up. He would instead point out the mistakes that I made or the inadequate work that I had done. If my work didn't match his expectation, then I could expect to be in trouble. This kind of conditioning can be carried around with us our entire lives if we fail to address the issue.

Getting back to my forklift abilities…If I had admitted that I had shoved the forks through the bags of fertilizer, then I would have been agreeing with my dad's assessment of my inadequacies. "I am not good enough; I failed yet again." I call this false thinking. Believing something untrue about ourselves will negatively affect us. Someone else can tell you that it isn't true, but you don't really believe them because of your past conditioning.

Excuses

What are some of the ways that we can avoid our responsibility? One way is by making excuses, which is what I did when I put the forks through the fertilizer and said, "It must have been delivered to us that way," or "I think that one of the other guys must not have been paying attention." We always have an excuse for whatever we do. Maybe you have been eating all the food that you shouldn't be eating: pizza, chips, ice cream, and chocolate. You justify wrong eating habits because of your job. Your boss has been on you lately or the workload has increased. The real reason is the food makes you feel better and brings you comfort. Perhaps you have been angry at your spouse and kids. Why? After a long day at work, you are tired and when you get home, you just want to relax. Your thinking says, *I don't need anyone bothering me. I just need some space right now. Why can't they understand that?*

When it comes to taking responsibility, I believe we are all tested when we are driving in traffic. I have a bad habit of talking to people in other cars when I see them do something that I don't agree with—even when I know they can't hear me! However, when I do something wrong on the road, I try to justify it by thinking, *It's okay. I'm late for an important meeting! Everyone else does it, so what's the big deal?*

One time when I was driving toward the mountain, out of nowhere blue lights start flashing behind me. I thought, *he must be after the car ahead of me.* Only he wasn't. I pulled over, and the officer asked me for my license and registration. "Do you know why I pulled you over?"

I said, "No."

"I clocked you going 15 miles over the speed limit."

I thought, *Big deal! Everyone does that!*

He went back to his car and wrote me out a ticket.

I couldn't believe he ticketed me! I never saw a speed limit sign the entire time I was on that road. I was going down a hill at the time he clocked me, and he wasn't even polite. I told everyone who would listen to me how unfair it was that I received a ticket. I stated in no uncertain terms, "I am going to go to court and tell the judge exactly what I think."

In the end, I went to court, but I didn't say anything in my defense. I paid the money. Just for fun, I looked up the top excuses given when pulled over by a police officer:

- "I couldn't see the sign."
- "I am lost and unfamiliar with the roads around here."

- "I didn't know that I broke the speed limit."
- "Everyone else is doing it."
- "I have an emergency situation in my car."

Maybe you have used one of these. I know I have. The reality is, the police officer has already heard your excuse dozens of times. Trying to escape responsibility doesn't help us move forward; it actually prevents our moving forward.

Denial

Another way that we avoid responsibility is denial, i.e., convincing ourselves and trying to convince others that we don't have a problem. Everyone around us notices the problem—except us. "Since I don't have a problem, I don't have to get help or change." Addicts use the defense mechanism of denial all the time. When I was meeting with a couple who had separated, the husband talked about the lack of trust that his wife had in him. She had apparently found evidence on his phone to make her forego her trust. While his wife sat quietly beside him listening, he continued to make his case for several minutes.

I finally told him that I wanted to hear from his wife. "I found him texting other women and looking at pornography," she simply stated.

He blustered, "It isn't any of her business…"

I interrupted him. "When you married her, your life became an open book. Why would you need to hide anything from your spouse unless you are guilty? I told him that my wife can look at my phone any time she wants because I have nothing to hide. Then I asked him, "Is what your wife told me true?"

He reluctantly said, "Yes, but I will stop."

When a person is *caught* instead of *coming clean*, there is a big difference when it comes to change. Often the person who is caught is either humbled or angry. When the person is caught, seeing lasting change can be tough. The *motivation* to change makes all the difference.

I have found that the best motivation comes when we desire to change ourselves. We come to the realization that we no longer want to live the way we were living. We no longer want to go around hiding. We don't want something to have control over us. When we are caught, we may feel remorseful, but our motivation to change our behavior comes from a couple of sources:

1. Wanting to make ourselves look better or feel better.
2. Wanting to make someone else happy

We must desire change because we see the need to change.

With the couple I was counseling, the husband had been caught, and he was in denial about his sin. I told him that if he wanted to save his marriage, he needed to seek help. Denial is a powerful force that can convince us that our behavior is acceptable, and our sin is not that big of a problem.

Minimizing

One last way that we skirt responsibility is by *minimizing*. In the story that I used to illustrate denial, the husband also tried to minimize what he had done. He said that the gal he was texting was "just a friend," and "There isn't anything inappropriate with texting a friend." He also said, "I only look at porn occasionally."

His minimizing his actions sounds so much better, doesn't it? Not! Married men and women don't have text conversations with the opposite gender without their spouse's knowing it. That basic rule of thumb even applies for business. If you must communicate regularly with the opposite gender, I would suggest that you copy or include your spouse anytime that you need to communicate with them, then you will avoid being tempted.

I cannot tell you how many marriages have been destroyed because of a relationship in business that starts innocently but without transparency. Minimizing convinces us that our behavior is not a problem, which often leads to a much bigger problem.

So why do we use excuses, denial and minimizing? Fear is one reason. If we admit or come clean, then we must face change, and making needed changes can be scary. The fear of the unknown can stop us even though we know we need to change. The other reason that we use to excuse our sinful behavior is that we like what we are doing. Our sin brings us some satisfaction. Unfortunately, the satisfaction is only temporary, but the temporary factor is not on our minds. Enjoying the pleasures of such sins as porn or drugs or alcohol or overeating can end up robbing us from the freedom that we desire.

Galatians 6:5 says, *"for we are each responsible for our own conduct."* Taking responsibility for our choices is crucial if we want to be set free. We are not responsible for anyone else, only ourselves, which means that we must understand how our choices have led us to where we currently are. And, if you are not satisfied with where you are, then you must take the proper responsibility for the actions that led you this place.

Action 2—Personal Assessment

For many years, part of my responsibility as a supervisor was to evaluate each of my team members in writing twice a year. Evaluations are designed to provide an assessment of how each person is performing in his job role. When I was younger, I lacked the ability and discernment to write evaluations that inspired them to be better employees; I tended to focus on the negatives more than the positives. The problem with that kind of evaluation is its lack of motivating; rather, it actually discourages the employee reading his evaluation. Who looks forward to receiving an evaluation full of negatives from the supervisor?

Taking a personal assessment is like an evaluation. We look at where we are at and how we got there. As we walk through this process, we may feel apprehensive about looking at our past. I mean, who wants to look back at all of their mistakes, failures, and pain? But taking a thorough look at our past, including the bad but also the good, is important.

For many years I never wanted to look at my past. In fact, when I thought about my childhood, I had very few memories. Seemingly, I had blocked them out of my mind. Later, I would learn that I had done exactly that. When we go through painful or traumatic events, our mind protects us by burying them in the deepest recesses, not eliminating the memories. We no longer acknowledge these hurts. I believe that many of the destructive behaviors and addictions people embrace are the direct result of these hidden hurts, which is why finding the pain agents from our past is so important.

Taking a personal assessment gives us a picture of our lives. The goal is not to bring guilt or shame upon us but to give us some markers upon which to build. Think about viewing your life in different stages like childhood, young adult, and adulthood. The following is an example from my own life.

My childhood was filled with painful events. When I was in elementary and middle school, I was ridiculed for being short. I was a late bloomer and didn't grow until my junior year in high school. It's sad to think that kids can be so cruel and unkind because of another person's height, weight or looks. When I was waiting at the bus stop, some kids would call me names and start pushing me to provoke a fight to prove that they were tougher than me. The point came when I decided to walk to school. Avoiding the bullies and walking was probably good for my physical conditioning, but my fear of bullies was sad. This is how rejection can impact our life.

When I was in the school band, a fellow student began hitting me in class. The matter all came down to my size, me being small than him. I played the trumpet, and so did he. The way that a musician is seated in the band is determined by the ability of the person and what instrument he plays. Every musician tries to advance to the coveted first chair. He and I, unfortunately, sat next to each other. I dreaded going to band class merely because of him. These examples are all traumatic events that can scar a young person.

On the flip side, I also enjoyed many positives while growing up. I mentioned that I played the trumpet, but playing the trumpet was my therapy. I would go to my room and play for a couple of hours every evening. I think my parents must have possessed great patience to listen to me for all those school years. Music can be such a gift, and it surely was for me. A couple of great memories involving music include marching in the Rose Parade in Portland and playing for the Portland Trailblazers after they won the NBA championship.

The other positive during my childhood was horticulture, the science or art of growing plants, which includes landscape and garden design as well as plant conservation. One of my friends, who had a greenhouse, peaked my interest in growing plants. I decided to build my own greenhouse, and the rest was history. In high school, I was in the horticulture class and a member of the horticulture team. I most remember my teachers in both band and horticulture. Their encouraging and supportive influence inspired me to make good choices when I could have selected the complete opposite.

Another part of life that we seldom consider is the ugly part—the pain-filled moments for which we were not responsible. Those choices made by others include our parents' divorce, a car accident or a medical condition.

What we need to do is to get a picture of the different significant events throughout our lives. A simple way is to take each stage or season of life and summarize the good, the bad and the ugly. This process is outlined in more detail in our Freedom workbook. The following chart is an example of what I am suggesting.

Season of Life	Good	Bad	Ugly
Childhood	won a spelling bee made all-star team	took first drink bullied by neighbor	parents' divorce
Young Adult	Graduated college	stole pornography started partying	victim in car accident

As you embrace this process, you can see the different events that have shaped you thus far in your life. Remember that as we take personal responsibility for the bad choices that we have made, we can also take credit for our right choices. I think that looking at the good is just as important because we can forget the many positives that we experienced.

The second part of the assessment stage is looking at the consequences of those significant events. For me, rejection was a negative consequence of the bullying that I experienced. A part of rejection is the lack of acceptance. I didn't feel like I was a part of my class; simply put, I felt like an outcast. When we are in school, we are shaped by what others say about us or how they treat us. The so-called cliques are present in every school as are the jocks, the stoners, and the geeks. Doesn't that sound like some positive role models?!

The few friends with whom I associated, like me, didn't really fit into any group. Perhaps you can relate when you think back to your days in school. Another negative consequence involved my self-worth. Because I was smaller than most kids, I felt like I did not measure up nor was good enough. At the time I didn't recognize the impact that a low self-worth would have on me. The majority of my memories involving school were not positive. The pain that I experienced didn't go away on its own; I had to take some action to be healed.

The final area to evaluate during the assessment stage is to consider the strengths and weaknesses of those significant relationships. Different people make different impacts on us— both good and bad. Though my relationship with my dad was not the best, I want to share some of the negatives and positives I learned from him.

My dad possessed the quality of commitment. He was married to my mom for over 50 years, and I have no memory of them ever discussing divorce. They did weather several fights through the years but it never escalated to separation. He worked at his job for over 25 years and never missed a day of work. Sadly, that kind of commitment is seldom seen anymore.

My father also owned the quality of dependability. Whenever someone asked my dad for help, he would be there. People knew they could always count on my dad. Part of his dependability involved being on-time, meaning he was early to everything. Dad considered himself late if he wasn't 30 minutes early.

Another strength my father passed on to me was honesty. I never remember my dad's saying something that later I found out to be untrue. He instilled in me that being less than honest wasn't an option.

Like every one of us, my father possessed some weaknesses as well. My dad never expressed love. I have no recollection of his ever saying, "I love you, son." I have learned that there is always a reason for our deficits. I found out later in life that my father did not have the most positive childhood. Both of his parents emigrated from Germany to North Dakota, where they married and raised twelve children. He never talked extensively about his childhood, except to say his father, whom I never knew, was a huge man who kept order by fear and intimidation. Dad once said that if you looked at his dad (my grandfather) the wrong way at the dinner table, he would backhand you across the room. That hard life could have been the catalyst behind his own anger issues and lack of love.

Dad's other compelling weakness was his lack of encouragement. Neither my sister nor I ever heard many words of encouragement while growing up. His expectations were many, but his words of admiration were few. Again, I am relatively sure that the reason came down to his lack of support growing up.

Recognizing how those significant relationships affect us is important. I can see the positive impact as well as the negative. If possible, a good exercise is to list your strengths and weaknesses inherited from your mother and your father. Then take an honest look at yourself and see if you see any similarities. The best result of undertaking this process is knowing that you can change! If you don't like something about yourself, don't give up. We can all change if we desire to change and will take the appropriate actions.

Action 3—Identify Attachments

As you look at the significant events and relationships throughout your life, you can see how they have shaped who you are. When Kathy and I welcomed our first child, I can remember the joy of holding our new baby; her skin was so soft, her hands and feet so small, and her smiles were like receiving a gift. The thought that she was a part of me was difficult to embrace. I loved holding her in my arms and talking to her—even though she couldn't understand what I was saying. Whenever I was at work, I couldn't wait to be with her again.

What happens with a baby and the parents is called bonding or forming an attachment? The child becomes attached to us, and we become attached to them. It is that bond that creates social, emotional and cognitive development. As we mature and develop in life, we also have attachments that are both healthy and unhealthy.

When we attach to something that is unhealthy, we give it power and control over us as well as providing us with a sense of safety or satisfaction. Attachments can happen with money, cars, drugs, alcohol, body image, food, relationships, and a host of other possible choices.

Because of my lack of love and encouragement growing up, I tried to find someone who could give me what I was missing. The obvious answer to me was a girl. I was 17 years old when I found my first serious girlfriend. We started hanging out, and our relationship soon turned physical. Yes, my hormones were amped up, but much more was going on than hormones. My attachment was based on my need for love. I was looking to a relationship to fill the emptiness inside of me. We were together for over a year, and during that time, I thought that everything was going well. One day she called to break up with me. I was shocked and couldn't believe what I was hearing.

When I look back now, I can clearly see how unhealthy our relationship had become. Inside of me, I still had that unmet need of love, so before long I was pursuing another girl. When we have an emptiness inside of us, we will continue to search for a way to fill that void. However, when we attach to something or someone, we can become dependent, giving control to that person or behavior. Addiction often begins this way.

Every attachment formed is an attempt to meet an unmet need in your life but forming attachments—healthy or unhealthy—cannot give you what you are looking for nor can they set you free. Only God can fill that void.

When we read the bible, there is much written about idols. An *idol* is something that we pursue, desire, love or worship, or anything that we look to satisfy us outside of God is considered an idol. The first of the Ten Commandments says that we are to have no other gods before Him. Following this commandment is important because only God can give us what we are seeking. God alone can meet the needs that we have and provide us with satisfaction. When we go to something or someone other than God it will ultimately bring us pain.

Looking at our desires can help us identify our attachments. Anything used to cope, escape to, seek comfort in, gain control, meet your needs or find your identity in would be classified as desires. For example, if I have a desire for money and I need to have more money, that desire can become unhealthy. My desire for money can become my security and influence my self-worth. I can feel good when I have enough money, but I can feel discouraged or even stressed when I do not have enough.

Take food, for example. Of course, we need to eat, but what if certain foods are all that we desire? When we eat them, it makes us feel good temporarily, and when we don't eat them, it affects not only how we feel but also our mood.

Desires like food and money can become unhealthy attachments. If you are like me, you can easily see how quickly our desires can become attachments. Taking this step will help you identify those things that are preventing you from having freedom. As you look over your life, do you recognize any unhealthy attachments? If so, then recognizing it as an attachment is the first step of breaking its power over you.

Action 4—Practice Transparency

Every year people spend millions of dollars buying costumes for themselves as well as for their pets. This spending frenzy happens every thirty-first day of October for, yes, you guessed it—Halloween. Whether you happen to agree with this holiday doesn't stop people from going crazy and sending their kids out in the "search" for candy. I was the kind of kid who tried to get as much candy as possible and then ration it over the next six months!

Where did Halloween originate anyway? This annual observance is actually an ancient Celtic holiday where people believed they needed masks to protect themselves from evil spirits that roamed the earth on All Hallows Eve. I want to focus on the mask part of Halloween.

People wear masks on more than just Halloween; in fact, people wear masks every day of the year. Of course, I am not referring to physical masks, but the invisible ones—the masks that we hide behind. Some hide behind emotional masks where we tell everyone that we are doing fine or good when, in reality, we are doing terrible. Have you ever used that one?

Some seek to hide behind the mask of joking or sarcasm. Others can hide behind the mask of anger or over-controlling, or the introvert or the social butterfly. Every person has his choice of dozens of masks to wear. Why do we put on these masks?

Simply put, we hide behind our masks because we don't want anyone knowing who we really are. For the most part, wearing masks comes from insecurity and pain. Our mask becomes our security and makes us feel safe. When our daughters were struggling with drug addiction, Kathy and I often wore our masks. People would ask, "How are your children doing?" and we would reply, "Everyone is doing well."

We didn't want anyone to know the real truth. Fear drives people to need a mask. The fear of looking like our lives was a complete mess or the fear of looking like a failure as a parent. These genuine thoughts and fears filled our minds. Not only do we wear these masks for our own protection, but they also become a wall between God and us. We put on our mask because we feel ashamed for what we have done.

The hidden things are what keep us chained. The answer is transparency. We make ourselves transparent by sharing with someone what we have done. Why? Because transparency and honesty will bring healing. Of course, sharing and being transparent with someone carries a risk, but the alternative is to carry the weight with us and continuously try to convince everyone that life is good. Part of the transparency process is finding someone whom we can trust, someone who we know is for us. We don't want someone who is critical or who will lecture us, they need to be a safe person. Once we find that person, we then tell them about our struggles and weaknesses.

In my role of pastor and speaking about all kinds of issues, I have had to determine how transparent I want or need to be. Sharing about every struggle in detail with a large group of people wouldn't be wise or beneficial. However, I also don't want to portray myself as being perfect and without problems either. My goal is to be real when I talk. If I have struggled with anger, then I will tell others about my struggle. If I have messed up my marriage, then I will let others know. If I have allowed pride to stop me from doing right, then I will say so. I have done all of those things. If you are looking for a perfect pastor or a perfect author, then you will not find one here.

For many years, pastors have put on a façade to give the impression that everything in their life is in perfect order and all is good. Unfortunately, so many have fallen to extramarital affairs, drug abuse and the misappropriation of money. Surveys have revealed that pastors are some of the loneliest people. They are so busy trying to help others that rarely are they helping themselves. Transparency is something that we all need, including pastors, to be healthy. Just imagine the weight that can be lifted by sharing your baggage with another person. Remember that transparency isn't a one and done confrontation; it's a discipline that we need to learn. Releasing the load that we carry is helpful and healing.

If you do not have someone in your life with whom you can share, I would encourage you to pray and ask God to show you that person. Taking ownership of our lives is essential in the pursuit of freedom. Honesty is our friend.

Action 5—Find Accountability

If you were to attend an AA meeting, you would be informed that finding a sponsor is an integral part of recovery. Why? There are a couple of reasons, but the primary one is support. A sponsor has also walked the road that you are walking. Sponsors understand the battle, and they know what it takes to experience victory. They come alongside you, are available whenever you need to talk, or need support. Knowing they are not there to judge or condemn you is so important. Having sponsors is invaluable to the success of AA's goals.

Transparency and accountability are closely linked. As we walk through the freedom process, we also need someone or a small group of individuals who can come alongside of us for accountability. Unfortunately, accountability partners can sometimes be viewed like a law enforcement officer's making sure that we are doing right and obeying the rules. If we don't obey, then the hammer comes down. Accountability partners get a bad rap! What is the truth?

We set up our own accountability rules, and we determine what our goals will be. The accountability partner will ask us how we are doing in attaining those goals. Depending on the issue, we will also set up the frequency of the check-ups. Accountability partners are also in place to encourage us and celebrate our victories. Our responsibility is telling the truth. The only way that accountability will be beneficial to us is if we are being honest.

A friend who was addicted to opiates asked me to be his accountability partner. Of course, I agreed to his request. I would see him each week at church and ask him how he was doing. He would tell me if he was doing good or if he was struggling. I also tried to connect with him during the week, but I started to see a difference in him. I felt like he was avoiding me or not telling me the real truth or the whole truth. My feelings were accurate; he was continuing to use, and his dishonesty eventually hurt him and his family. My job wasn't to make sure he was being honest; it was his. His lack of honesty prevented me from helping him. It didn't mean that I wasn't concerned for him; it just meant that I could only do my part.

Let me share a personal example. If my goal is to stop overreacting and getting angry at my children, then my accountability partner might ask me daily how I am doing.

That check-in can be a phone call or, at the very least, a brief text message. Knowing that I will be asked about my anger issue will hopefully stop me before I overreact. But if I do overreact in anger, I can be assured that my partner will not put me down for what I have done. This keeps our relationship healthy. An element of safety is a must in accountability.

I have been a part of several accountability groups in my life, and from firsthand experience, I can testify that they are beneficial. In one of the groups, I met with three other men.

When the four us decided to meet together, we each shared a different struggle that we were working to overcome. We checked on each other throughout the week and physically met together on Wednesday mornings. Knowing that I would be asked about my anger issues helped my awareness of my problem throughout the week. I cannot stress enough that the person or persons whom you choose for accountability partners need to be healthy spiritually. I am not saying that they are perfect and have no issues, but they are supportive, encouraging, respectful, honest, and trustworthy. Share your goals and then come to an agreement on how often you desire to be contacted.

Let me share one important thing when it comes to accountability partners. I believe that they need to be of the same gender. A married couple can conveniently use a spouse as an accountability partner, but I don't believe it is the best. I can testify from personal experience that this situation can cause conflict and stress on the marital relationship. A husband should not put his spouse in that role and vice versa. The same is true with singles. My recommendation would always be to find an accountability partner in the same gender.

Think about these questions;

If you knew that someone would be asking you about overeating, would it make you think before you took that bite?

If you knew that someone would be asking you about looking at porn, would it make you think twice before bringing up that site?

If you knew that someone would be asking you about your gambling or your shopping or your video gaming, would it stop you before doing what you know you shouldn't be doing?

That is the power of accountability.

King Solomon writes about this power in the book of Ecclesiastes:

Two people are better off than one, for they can help each other succeed. If one person falls, the other can reach out and help. But someone who falls alone is in real trouble. Likewise, two people lying close together can keep each other warm. But how can one be warm alone? A person standing alone can be attacked and defeated, but two can stand back-to-back and conquer. Three are even better, for a triple-braided cord is not easily broken (Ecclesiastes 4:9-12)

According to these verses, we are stronger together than we are alone. One of the most significant risks that we can ever take is reaching out to another person and sharing our struggles. But one of the greatest rewards in life comes when we take that risk. The freedom process is built on accountability. This person or persons is critical to our success.

Chapter 3
THE CHOICE
TO HEAL

Pain is discomfort that we will all experience at some time in life. Often when we feel pain, our first response is to get rid of it. But pain is God's way of sending us a message. Ignoring it or trying to move on often means facing more pain and complications.

Last year my wife and I were on a short getaway in Santa Fe, New Mexico, and during our first night, something didn't feel quite right. I felt a terrible pain in my side, and no matter what I tried, the pain didn't subside. I finally decided to go to the urgent care and find out what was happening. The doctor on duty ordered some tests to check for possible kidney stones and ultimately told me that he believed I had an infection. He gave me a prescription for some medication, and I went to the pharmacy. Within a day or two, the pain had left. What could have happened if I had decided to ignore the pain would have been a hospital stay. Physical pain is no different than emotional or relational pain; we still must find the cause to receive the right treatment.

The first year after I moved to Albuquerque, a man stopped at our church, wanting to speak with a pastor. I was available, so I went to meet the man and invite him to my office. He didn't attend our church but was driving by, saw our sign, and something deep inside of him said to turn in, so he did. I could tell that he was troubled, but he composed himself and began telling me a little about his life. "I believe in God," he shared, but he didn't elaborate on his relationship with God and proceeded to tell me that he had been married for over 20 years, and he was in sales. "My job often sends me around the country, and on one of my trips, I met a woman at an airport while we were waiting for our flights. We exchanged phone numbers, made plans to communicate, and within a short time, we set up a meeting. Our acquaintance soon moved into a physical relationship. I've been seeing this other woman for a couple of years."

I asked, "Have you told your wife?"

"I will never tell her, and I will take this secret to my grave," he said.

I shared with him what the consequences of his decision would mean. I realized the man had no interest in listening to me nor any desire to receive counsel nor to make changes in his lifestyle. He finished telling me what he had been carrying around with him, and then stood up and left. I never saw the man again. I guess he felt like he needed to confess this deep, dark secret to a pastor. Unfortunately, I couldn't give him what he was looking for.

Statistics reveal that 22 percent of married men and 14 percent of married women have committed adultery. What happened to the vows and promises that they made to each other on their wedding day? What brought them to believe that this other person would meet their needs better than their spouse?

I have the privilege of meeting with couples who are planning to marry. I meet with the couple for several sessions and try to share essential tools that will help them prepare for their marriage. One of the questions that I usually ask is about any previous relationships. I want to know about their longest relationship and how it ended. Checking to see if there was closure so that the person can move forward is absolutely essential. One of the primary reasons for ending a relationship is broken trust. One person cheated on the other one. When trust has been broken in a relationship, more trust issues are generally created.

A friend of mine was having trouble in his marriage. He decided to seek help from a therapist, who asked him to bring his wife with him for the next appointment. His wife came with him as requested. As the therapist began talking to the wife, she became increasingly defensive and hostile. "*I* don't have any problems; this is all my husband's fault!" She walked out of the appointment and never came back. Her main issue with her husband was trust. She believed that he was sleeping with numerous women. He completely denied her accusations. She had never seen anything to validate what she believed—no text messages or phone calls; she only had *a feeling*. When he and I talked about their marriage, he shared that she had been married before, and her ex-husband had been unfaithful on numerous occasions.

What do we do when we encounter pain as the result of a relationship? Unfortunately, moving on isn't a good answer. Pain doesn't go away on its own; it must be healed. Looking at our past can be one of the best ways to help prepare us for the future. We have a choice to heal. Healing is process that every one of us needs. Trying to forget our past would seem an easy choice; unfortunately, that pain goes along with us wherever we go—like carrying along an extra suitcase. Some of us are holding on tightly to this *baggage*.

I am reminded of attending a conference in Idaho with five other pastors from our church. When we landed at the Spokane Airport, we stopped by the restroom and took our time before heading to the baggage claim. I have found when you rush to get your bags, you end up waiting anyway. We arrived, and everyone grabbed his or her bag but me. I waited and waited for more luggage to arrive as I watched the only bag left continuing to circle the claim area belt. The black bag looked like mine, but it clearly wasn't mine.

That's when it hit me! *Someone has grabbed my bag, thinking it was theirs.* My fellow pastors and I went over to the baggage claim representative and explained what we thought had happened. She checked the only piece of luggage, found the name of the owner on the tag, and called her. The lady didn't realize what had happened, and fortunately, she hadn't left the airport. She came back, and we exchanged bags. The moral of the story? When the flight attendant tells you to make sure that you check your bag before taking it, listen!

Why do I share this story? When I couldn't find my bag, a sinking feeling hit the pit of my stomach. I thought, *staying in Idaho for three days with only the clothes on my back would not be good! What will I do without my stuff—the stuff that I am familiar with.* The baggage or the pain of the past that we carry around similarly affects us. Our pain becomes our friend; it's what we know. When we think about getting rid of it, fear can overwhelm us. *How can I live without it? How will I manage?* And my response to those questions would be—freedom!

In life, relationships often bring hurt. No matter how careful we are, someone is likely to hurt us, and we are likely to hurt someone. So how do we heal from this pain? The following are some actions to take.

Action 1—Learn Forgiveness

When I was a child, I would listen to my parents' fight. Thankfully, their quarrels didn't happen that often, but when they did, everyone could hear. The yelling didn't last too long, but then the silence would begin. My parents wouldn't speak with each other for several days sometimes.

During my childhood, I never remember hearing them apologize to one another, and I never heard them reconciling their differences. The word *reconcile* is a word that is seldom used in normal conversation except by an accountant or a Christian. The word simply means to "restore a relationship." We often learn how to fight or how to reconcile from our parents. In fact, both Kathy and I surely did. The undeniable truth is, none of us is perfect, and because of that lack of perfection, each one of us sins or disobeys God. Because of that sin, each of us has been separated from God. When Jesus came to the earth and gave His life up for us, He paid the penalty for our sin. When we accept Christ's gift of salvation, we are reconciled to God or restored to Him.

When someone causes us pain, the way to heal from that betrayal is to forgive. Unfortunately, I have found that there are many misunderstandings when it comes to forgiveness.

Several years ago, Kathy and I were friends with another couple, whom I will call the Smiths, from our church. They were members of our small group, and we met with them and others once a week to study the Bible, eat, and do life together. As our friendship with the Smiths grew, our families would get together to enjoy activities. Mr. Smith had been in a terrible car accident that resulted in a head injury, which affected his speech and his ability to walk. For him to pick up his one foot was difficult. This large man, who stood around six foot three and weighed over two hundred pounds, had always been friendly, but something about him didn't seem quite right.

After knowing the Smiths for a couple of years, I arrived at church one Sunday morning, where I was met by the pastor.

Without much small talk, he asked, "Could you come into a room with me?"

When I walked into the room, I was shocked to see all of the church leadership sitting in a circle with our friends, the Smiths.

The pastor said, "Mr. Smith is accusing you of having an affair with his wife."

When I heard that statement, I was relieved and started laughing. "Is this some kind of joke?"

"No, but he really believes this accusation."

"I have never done anything inappropriate with his wife nor have I ever intended to! What did Mrs. Smith say?

The pastor said, "Mrs. Smith has denied that anything happened. In fact, she was thoroughly embarrassed that this whole accusation has been brought before the church."

"What evidence does Mr. Smith have?"

"Well, none."

In other words, he was only accusing me of something that he believed was true. The frightening part of his accusation was he truly believed his wife and I were having an affair, and there was no convincing him differently. Apparently, his head injury had affected more than his leg; his mind had also been affected, and the problem was becoming worse. I would love to say that everyone just moved on from this situation, but it didn't.

A few weeks had passed when I learned that he was parking on our street, watching our house. One evening I heard a knock at our door, and when I opened the door, Mr. Smith was standing there. "I was just driving by," he explained, "and I wanted to ask you what you thought about me buying a firearm."

I immediately knew he wasn't simply driving by because he lived on the complete opposite side of the city. I knew he was sending me a strong message. The threats someone makes on your life and your family is not easily forgiven. Our friendship had ended.

I have shared this story to illustrate the importance of forgiveness—the act of releasing or pardoning an offender. Forgiveness has less to do with the other person and more to do with us. Forgiving frees us from the control of the other person. When we say that we will not forgive someone, what we are really saying is that we won't set ourselves free. In the account involving Mr. Smith, I had every right to say, "I will not forgive him." We didn't do anything wrong; all we did was extend the hand of friendship.

When we fail to forgive, we are making a choice to keep ourselves in prison. And that prison will have walls of resentment and bitterness. I really believe that we don't truly understand what forgiveness is and what it isn't. Let me start by sharing what forgiveness isn't.

- It's not pretending you're not hurt.
- It's not saying that what the person did was acceptable.
- It's not saying that there won't be consequences, depending on what the person did.
- It doesn't mean that your relationship goes back to normal because the person may not be safe.
- It doesn't mean that we won't be hurt or that we will simply forget everything.
- And it doesn't mean that they deserve your forgiveness.

Unfortunately, we seldom see the act of forgiveness modeled for us in the world. Many times, we see the complete opposite with people wanting to get even or looking for payback. In fact, Hollywood loves to produce movies about revenge. Without much thought, I can readily think of *Payback, Gladiator, Taken, John Wick* and *Unforgiven*. Something inside of us connects with a good revenge story. However, when we look in the Bible, we see the complete opposite is true. Forgiveness equals freedom.

Remember that with forgiveness comes healing. I really believe that we must receive forgiveness first and understand its meaning before we can forgive someone else.

Action 2—Receive Forgiveness

A woman came to my office and shared with me that her husband was addicted to methamphetamines. This dangerous, potent drug is very difficult to defeat. After numerous attempts of trying to overcome his addiction on his own, his wife found a rehab center, where he stayed for four months. This rehab center, like many others cost several thousands of dollars. But just because you pay more does not guarantee positive results. Sadly, when her husband returned home, he started using again in two days.

Many times, addiction is viewed as destroying the person (which it does), but a ripple effect also takes place. The family is often forgotten in addiction. The pain, the dishonesty, and the broken trust makes a lasting impact. When it comes to addiction, there are no winners.

In my mind, the bigger question is whether he had realized how much he had hurt his wife and family. Sadly, the answer to that question was no. According to *dictionary. com, addiction* is "defined as the state of being enslaved to a habit or practice or to something that is psychologically or physically habit-forming as narcotics, to such an extent that its cessation causes severe trauma." The choices that we make lead to the actions that we take, and those actions can and will lead to pain when they stem from selfish desire. When that man finally breaks that meth addiction in his life, how hard will it be for him to receive forgiveness from his family and those he has hurt?

Every one of us has made choices that we wish we could go back and change. I wish that I could go back and change the way that I treated my wife and children. I wish I could change the many unhealthy relationships that I had because I was the main reason that they were unhealthy. I wish that I could change all the hurt that I caused so many people. We can be the most difficult person to forgive. When we cannot forgive ourselves, then often we turn to something that will help us escape or temporarily take away our pain. This solution only leads to more problems, more guilt, and additional shame. The only way to be truly free is by receiving forgiveness.

There is a story in the Bible where Jesus is teaching about forgiveness. Jesus was having dinner with a religious leader, and a prostitute walked into the house and began to clean His' feet. For the host to clean his guest's feet because they would be dirty from traveling in sandals was customary in Bible days. However, this religious leader never offered and became disgusted by the woman cleaning His feet. Because of her past, he could not believe that Jesus would allow this kind of woman to touch Him. It is easy for us to do the same thing today, isn't it? We can put people in different categories by what they own, where they work, how they look, or what they have accomplished.

Jesus then says the following:

> *"I tell you, her sins—and they are many—have been forgiven, so she has shown me much love. But a person who is forgiven little shows only a little love."* [48] *Then Jesus said to the woman, "Your sins are forgiven."*
> Luke 7:47-48 (NLT)

Did you catch what Jesus said? The one who has been forgiven much will show much love, but the one who has been forgiven little will love little. Personally receiving forgiveness will change us when we understand the wonderful gift we have been given.

Forgiveness begins with understanding what Jesus has done for us. Whenever we sin—disobey God—a payment must be made. Jesus gave the ultimate payment by giving His life. His payment paid for all of our sins—past, present, and future. So, when someone says, "God could never forgive me for what I have done in my past," that person is saying that Christ's sacrifice wasn't enough.

Forgiveness isn't earned; we cannot do enough to pay the price for our sins, but we don't need to. Chapter 1 addressed accepting the gift that God offers us, receiving eternal life, a new identity, and forgiveness. When we say, "God could never forgive me," we are placing ourselves to a higher standard then God does. The choice is really ours. It's not that God won't forgive us; it's that we won't accept His forgiveness. I hope that you will.

How Do We Accept His Forgiveness?

First, we admit what we have done, which is *confession*, i.e., "saying the same thing or agreeing with God." For example, it's saying, "I have sinned against You, God, for looking at porn today." "I sinned against You, God, when I slept with Susan years ago." "I sinned against You, God, when I lost my temper and yelled at my daughter."

Next, we turn away from what we have done. Remember as a child when you did something that you knew was wrong, and your mom or dad caught you? You probably used the same word I used: "Sorry!" The question that begs to be answered is are we sorry because we got caught, or are we sorry because of what we have done?

When we turn away from what we have done, our heart no longer wants to continue doing the same thing repeatedly.

Finally, we ask God to forgive us. The really good news is He promises to forgive us and cleanse us when we ask! I have a whiteboard mounted in my office, and as I plan different tasks, I add them to my board. After a couple of months, the board starts looking very busy or messy as I have written reminders in red, green and black markers. When I finish a task, I spray a solution on the board that wipes away my reminders, and nothing but a clean whiteboard remains. Having nothing written on the board feels so good!

When we confess our sins to God, He cleanses our heart and makes it as clean as fresh snow. King David in the Bible trusted in God and enjoyed great success as a king. With success, we oftentimes relax and start depending on ourselves more than God. The same was true of David, who should have left the comforts of the palace and personally led his troops to battle. Instead, he stayed home, and one afternoon as David was walking and relaxing on his patio rooftop, he noticed a beautiful woman taking a bath. He should have looked the other way, but he looked for a while. One bad decision can lead to another and down the rabbit hole we go. David sends for the woman and then sleeps with her.

This story only gets worse from this point. The woman was married, and her husband is away fighting for the king, yes the king who just slept with his wife. David then has the husband go to the front lines of the battle and then tells his general to pull back the troops. He was killed.

When we do things that we know were wrong our response is to cover up and lie. That is what King David did. No matter who we are, God sees each one of us the same, and He knows what we have done. He sent Nathan, His messenger, to confront the king with the truth. I want you to read what David wrote right after he was confronted by Nathan and as you do, look for his understanding of who God is and his understanding of forgiveness.

Have mercy on me, O God, because of your unfailing love. Because of your great compassion, blot out the stain of my sins. ²Wash me clean from my guilt. Purify me from my sin. ³For I recognize my rebellion; it haunts me day and night. ⁴Against you, and you alone, have I sinned; I have done what is evil in your sight. You will be proved right in what you say, and your judgment against me is just. ⁵For I was born a sinner—yes, from the moment my mother conceived me. ⁶But you desire honesty from the womb, teaching me wisdom even there. ⁷Purify me from my sins, and I will be clean; wash me, and I will be whiter than snow. ⁸Oh, give me back my joy again; you have broken me—now let me rejoice. ⁹Don't keep looking at my sins. Remove the stain of my guilt. ¹⁰Create in me a clean heart, O God. Renew a loyal spirit within me. (Psalm 51:1-10)

No matter what you have done, God's forgiveness is always readily available. After receiving forgiveness, it then becomes much easier to forgive others.

Action 3—Forgive Others

Ask almost anyone what sin is the most difficult to forgive, and adultery will always be at the top of that list.

A man who requested an appointment with me said that he was experiencing a crisis in his marriage. He had discovered that his wife had been seeing another man and was planning to leave him. "Will your wife come in and talk to me?" I asked.

"I will try to get her to come," he said.

One day later they made an appointment with me and came in together. He started by sharing all of the evidence that he found against his wife. She sat quietly listening to his open-and-shut case.

After listening to his side of the story for several minutes, I said, "Please quit talking about all this evidence. I now want to hear your wife's side of the story." I have learned through years of counseling with couples that there are always two sides of the story.

She said, "I have been asking him to go with me for marriage counseling for the last couple of years. Each time

I asked, he would make excuses, and things would level off in our marriage. But with every fight, the wall between us would get higher and higher. Eventually, I met another man who showed some interest in me. We began to connect at an emotional level, and I realized I was missing that kind of connection from my husband. Once my focus changed to this other man, he began noticing that something was wrong". She then added, "Nothing physical ever happened between us."

Again, I have learned that what is stated as fact is often not all of the truth, so I suggested, "I believe you should stop all communication with this other man."

She agreed. A few weeks went by, but I soon found out that she was still seeing the other guy, and their relationship was based on more than just meeting emotional needs. They had progressed to a physical relationship. Not only was there pain in the marriage, but they also had a couple of children who were also affected. How can we forgive someone who has wounded us like this? Forgiveness starts with a choice, and that choice brings freedom. Always remember that forgiveness is for our own benefit.

When we forgive another person, we are actually releasing ourselves from the other person's control. Both Kathy and I came from families that held on to the hurt that was caused by others. We both had aunts and uncles who did not talk to each other for several years.

Unforgiveness changes us, but not for the better; a lack of forgiveness brings resentment and bitterness. What often happens is that the person talks about the offense over and over again. Our family members did precisely that. They couldn't release the offense, and they were the ones who ended up changing. When I meet people who are very angry and very critical of others, typically an element of unforgiveness can be found inside of them.

How Do We Forgive the People Who Have Hurt Us?

We begin by naming the person and identifying what he or she has done to us. This step may sound obvious, but thinking about the matter is important. I had a boss who would say one thing to one person and then say something entirely different to another. He was a people pleaser who wanted everyone to like him. Sadly, he couldn't remember what he told each person. His lack of integrity became very frustrating. When I found out that he was talking about me behind my back and putting me down, I was very hurt. So, what exactly did he do to me? He lied to me, and he gossiped about me.

Maybe your parents divorced when you were young, and you still feel abandoned by them. Or perhaps your friend in school choose to hang out with other kids instead of you, and you felt rejection. The long list of hurts ranges from a broken trust to abuse to disrespect. Name the person and what wrong the person has done to you.

The next step is asking yourself what the person owes you. Whenever someone hurts us, he or she owes us something. I believe my former boss owed me the truth and an apology for talking about me behind my back. Parents who separated or divorced possibly owe their children a childhood. Other common answers include respect or love or an explanation.

Next, we give up the right to get even or to hold on to unforgiveness. This step is essential because we are releasing the other person. This step is also challenging because we want to hold on to that hurt or we want them to pay for hurting us. In other words, we want justice! Again, I want to emphasize that forgiving someone is for our benefit. Unfortunately, I have seen far too many people talking about another person in their past for decades. Why? Because they haven't forgiven them; and therefore, they are bound to them.

The final step in forgiveness is saying and meaning the words, "I forgive you." We must remember what Christ has done for us through forgiveness, and when we do, forgiving becomes much more comfortable. Colossians 3:13 says, *"Make allowance for each other's faults and forgive anyone who offends you. Remember, the Lord forgave you, so you must forgive others."* Why would we make allowance for each other's faults? How would we do that? We start by remembering that we are all imperfect, and we are going to do and say things that hurt one another. Then it's admitting that we are all sinners, and we all fall short of God's standard.

Next, the verse says to forgive anyone who offends you. How often are we offended by another person? All the time! Perhaps someone speaks harshly or doesn't listen to what we are saying. The chances are very real that each one of us will be offended often, so why should we forgive someone who has hurt us or offended us? We remember that God has forgiven us so we must forgive others. When we forgive another person, we are reflecting God's character in us. All of the things that we have done or said that we know were wrong, God has forgiven us. Notice that forgiving others is not merely a suggestion; it's a command. God's commands are for our benefit.

Before continuing, I want to address what to do if the person who has hurt us is no longer living? I recommend going through the same steps and adding the following: write a letter to the person. Think about what that person did to you, what he or she owes you, and then try to express giving up the right to get even. Finally, write out the words, "I forgive you." Another effective step in the forgiveness process is to place a chair in front of you and read the letter out loud as if the person was sitting in the chair. This action can and will bring great healing. God does not want us to be chained by the hurt of another person. He wants us to be free. Forgiving another person heals our heart and sets us free.

Action 4—Ask for Forgiveness

So far this chapter has addressed what forgiveness is and what it is not, as well as accepting God's forgiveness and forgiving those who have hurt us. When it comes to this choice of healing, one more area needs to be addressed: asking forgiveness from those I have hurt. This process can be quite challenging. The reason that we ask for forgiveness is to take responsibility for our actions and heal the relationship whenever possible.

My daughter and I had a conflict over a boundary that my wife and I had set with her and she did not like it. At this writing, she is 21 years old and not really progressing in her life. She works in a dead-end job, does not want to further her education, nor figure out what she wants to do. She pays for her car insurance and her phone, then wastes the rest of her money on whatever. We set a boundary requiring her to pay rent immediately if she did not go to college. With each passing month, her rent will increase. Doesn't it sound like we are mean parents? Of course, our desire was to motivate her to do something.

Her first response was anger. "It's not fair!" she exploded. "I'm going to move out."

"Okay, move out," we responded.

She quickly discovered that she didn't make enough money to leave home, so she was stuck.

At this point is when the conflict started. She began to question me about how unfair her mother and I were being. I didn't back down, but she didn't either. After questioning me for the fourth time, my voice also became louder. I should have stepped aside, ending the confrontation, but I didn't. I yelled at her, and she stomped off into her room. Was I wrong? Yes and no. I wasn't wrong for setting the boundary, but I was wrong for yelling at her in frustration.

After cooling off, we both met together and apologized. I could have easily made excuses and tried to justify my actions, but I was clearly wrong. When I told her I was wrong for yelling and becoming angry, our relationship was restored.

The good news is our daughter decided on what she wanted to do and applied for school. She started the week that I am writing these words.

In the Bible, Jesus gives an example of asking for forgiveness that I want to share.

> *"So if you are presenting a sacrifice at the altar in the Temple and you suddenly remember that someone has something against you, 24leave your sacrifice there at the altar. Go and be reconciled to that person. Then come and offer your sacrifice to God."*
> (Matthew 5:23-24)

In this day and age, most of us are not presenting a sacrifice at the altar of the temple, but we may go to church and offer a sacrifice of praise as we are singing songs to God. The point of this example is the urgency that is expressed. We need to go immediately to be reconciled to that person. As I have already stated, the word *reconcile* means "to restore." Our goal should be to repair the relationship with the other person. This reconciliation is not dependent on the other person's response; this attempt is our responsibility to do right.

The other person may not want to forgive you, but that is his or her choice. Now I believe I understand what you are likely feeling, and I know what you are thinking: *It's been so long ago. What good will it do? They won't understand. They don't even live around here anymore.* Everything within us says not to take this step of healing, but if we want to experience freedom and healing, then we need to do what God tells us to do. Our responsibility is to own what we have done.

Some Practical Steps on How to Ask for Forgiveness

Start with humility, trying not to make excuses or rationalizing our actions. We must communicate what we have done. Perhaps you have struggled with some sort of addiction, and you know that you have hurt your spouse or your parents or another person. Think about all the possible ways that you have hurt these loved ones—lying, mistrust, hiding sin, and causing them pain. This is what you want to express when you ask for forgiveness.

Another common example would be relationship pain. If you experienced a divorce or a bad break up or conflict with a relative, if at all possible, the goal is always to restore the relationship. Whenever relational conflict takes place, there will be hurtful words, perhaps gossip or wrongful judgment and then specific unhealthy actions. Again, think about what you did wrong and express that wrongdoing to the other person. Again, you cannot control the person's reaction, but you can do right and leave the rest or the results up to God. If the person doesn't want to forgive you, then that person will have to live with unforgiveness.

I would always say that the best way to ask for forgiveness is in person. The way that you approach the person will help determine how the person will accept what you say. If it is not possible to talk with the person face to face, then I would suggest either a phone call or a letter. If the situation is very sensitive, I would ask another person for clarity on how to proceed. For example, if you were involved with abuse in some way, then approaching that person could be very traumatic. I would either suggest having a third party with you when asking for forgiveness or writing a letter, and in that letter, offering to have a meeting with them if they would feel comfortable. Then, the person can make the decision based upon how he or she wants to proceed.

Asking for forgiveness is a choice that will bring healing. (In our workbook, we lay out a plan that helps with each of these areas that have been addressed in this chapter.)

Chapter 4
THE CHOICE TO GROW

Living in New Mexico is much different than living in the state of Washington. What I love about New Mexico is the 300-plus days of sunshine that we enjoy yearly, but when it only rains a few inches every year, there can be a deficit of green. New Mexico is called "the land of brown" for a reason! Most of the yards in Albuquerque are xeriscape, a landscape design that uses drought-tolerant plans that requires little to no supplemental water. The yards have very little grass and lots of rocks to help with water conservation. Our climate is arid with very little humidity—except during the monsoon season in July and August.

The weather pattern brings thunderstorms that have the potential of dumping an abundance of rain in a short amount of time. An exciting thing happens during this season: thousands of small weeds start popping up among the rocks. The rain and warm weather make a perfect environment for growth. Homeowners can find the "monsoon season" very challenging. I must pick or spray the weeds each week. If I don't, then I will have a green yard in no time, and it won't be grass. With the right ingredients, growth can happen even when we don't want it.

When I was a teenager, growing plants was really a passion in my life. I built my own greenhouse when I was only fifteen years old. I found learning about the different kinds of plants and what specific needs they had fascinating. All plants need certain elements to grow, including light, water, nutrients, proper temperature, and oxygen. My job was to make sure that each plant had what was needed. Each day when I arrived home from school, I would go to my greenhouse to check on all of my plants. Strange as it may sound, they were like family to me. Looking back on those days, I really believe that growing plants was therapeutic for me; the greenhouse was my escape. Once I learned how to grow the different plants, I would sell them throughout my neighborhood.

After I graduated from high school, I decided to go to the community college in our city and take every class offered concerning horticulture. I remember attending my first class in college and meeting my instructor, whose name was Herb Orange. (You can't make things like this up. With a name like that he was destined to work with plants.) What I really liked about Herb was his love for plants. When a teacher or instructor is passionate about what he is teaching, his passion is infectious. I attended college for two years, and my goal was to work as a landscape designer or in the horticulture field. These were my plans, but Proverbs 16:9 states, *"We can make our plans, but the Lord determines our steps."* During this time the country's economy was in terrible shape, and finding a good paying job proved difficult. On top of my plans, I had met the girl who would become my wife, and the rest is history. My career soon took a different direction.

Growth is an essential part of life. We are meant to grow. If we do not grow, we become unhealthy and stagnant. When I was a young boy, I would go to a marshy area close to our house where stagnant water could be found in small little puddles. I can still remember the noxious smell of those pools of water and the multiple bugs swimming in them. My friends and I would play around the water, but we knew that we could never drink it.

When things become stagnant, nothing good ever comes from it. If we do not grow, then we become similar to those stagnant pools of water. We start stinking, and no one wants to be around us. Growth requires the right ingredients, like wisdom, truth, honesty, and desire, to name a few. Growing doesn't simply happen on its own; it is a choice that we make. Growth needs to happen in every area of our lives—emotionally, physically, relationally, intellectually, and spiritually. Over the last several years, I have found some significant action steps that have helped me in the area of growth that I would like to share.

Action 1—Change Our Thinking

For the majority of my life, I tried to stop allowing my anger to control me. I studied anger, and I read books on how to manage my anger. Though taking these steps was helpful, my anger was never fully gone. I would pray, asking God to change me and to take away the anger, but still, I seemed to get upset, and my struggles with anger continued. I felt like there was no hope for me at all. And then I remember picking up my Bible and reading this verse from the book of Romans: *"I don't really understand myself, for I want to do what is right, but I don't do it. Instead, I do what I hate"* (Romans 7:15). I felt as if the verse was speaking about me and my struggle. I wanted to do what is right, but instead, I did what I hated. Have you ever felt like that about yourself? What can we do?

I was sitting at my desk at work one day when I received an e-mail about a workshop that was coming to Portland, Oregon. The title of the workshop indicated that it would focus on helping others with addiction, which was right up my alley. I was always willing to learn about better ways that could help me to be more effective in my ministry. The workshop started on a Monday morning and ended on Friday afternoon. I registered for the conference and marked it on my calendar. Finally, the day arrived, and I was excited to learn how to help others. I headed to the conference center—an old, weathered building that wasn't much to look at.

I wondered if I had made the right choice. As I walked through the door, I saw rows of chairs with an aisle down the middle. I sat in the third row from the front on the right side. The man who led the workshop was kind of rough-looking, and he was definitely a black-and-white person. In fact, the way that he communicated was somewhat intimidating. After talking for several minutes, he handed out the material and began to work through it.

He shared that his knowledge of addiction came from years of personal experience. "I tried virtually every drug at one time or another as I was searching for my purpose in life. I studied and practiced many religions but never found what I was looking for." Eventually he discovered Christianity and became a follower of Christ. He began going to school, focusing on helping people with addictions. What he found was that many of the programs he worked with didn't see lasting change, and the majority of people returned to their addiction. As he studied further, he developed a different process that he believed could help others. He was given the opportunity to put his process into practice when he was hired to oversee a recovery center. Over the next few years, the results that he saw were incredible. Many of what he had learned and implemented was shared with those who attended the conference.

He did not speak in a polished manner, but I realized that what he was saying made more and more sense. As each hour passed, I became convinced that I had made the right decision to attend. My goal in going was to learn how to help others and to become more effective. But the longer I sat there, I began to realize that I was the one who needed to listen. I learned that my thinking was the key to real change. What we believe affects how we think, how we think affects how we feel, how we feel affects what we do, and what we do will produce the outcomes of our lives. If we don't like what is happening in our life, then we need to go all the way back to our beliefs.

As I sat in that workshop, I started to reflect on my anger and what was really causing it. Anger comes from pain, and most of the time, it tracks back to our past. Mine was no different, and I could see how my childhood was the culprit. During the week I was able to identify some of the false beliefs that originated when I was only a boy.

One false belief was never feeling like I could measure up or not feeling good enough. I already mentioned that my father had high expectations for my sister and me. If things were not done to his expectations, then we would get in trouble. We received little to no encouragement. This false belief was also reinforced by a couple of my schoolteachers, who were anything but positive and supportive. They only seemed to focus on my mistakes.

Another false belief was believing I must have respect to know I have value. When I was growing up, I never felt respected. To a man, I would say that respect is one of the most essential needs that we have. My dad never showed me respect by the way that he talked or treated me. My schoolmates didn't show me respect by teasing me or saying hurtful comments. And several of my employers failed to show me any respect. Embracing a false belief will have a negative impact on our life.

I realized that these false beliefs had really damaged my thinking. Whenever I felt like I didn't measure up to a certain standard, I would become angry. My anger wasn't necessarily displayed outwardly, but inside I became angry because of the reinforcement of my false belief that I wasn't good enough. If someone didn't show me respect, then I would immediately get angry because their actions reminded me of having no value.

In fact, this lack of respect was one trigger in our marriage. All of the baggage that I carried around with me followed me into our marriage relationship. Of course, Kathy had no idea what emotional baggage I was carrying. Whenever she would say something that seemed disrespectful to me, I would get angry at her. Whenever she would give permission to the kids without asking me, I would get angry. It's no wonder that everything I tried to do in my own power to eliminate my anger never worked.

Recognizing false beliefs is critical when it comes to real change and real freedom. The Bible contains some valuable verses that address our thinking. Romans 12:2 says, *"Don't copy the behavior and customs of this world, but let God transform you into a new person by changing the way you think. Then you will learn to know God's will for you, which is good and pleasing and perfect."* According to this verse, how are we changed? We change the way that we think. The word *transform* has the meaning of renovation. To *renovate* something is to make it new. We had our bathroom renovated a few years ago, and the process was absolutely awful. Everything was a complete mess, and the construction dust was everywhere. We couldn't use our shower for a couple of weeks as the floor was ripped up, and even some of our walls were torn apart. But when the renovation was complete, the bathroom looked amazing. Any evidence of the old bathroom was long gone!

This renovation process is a picture of our lives. When we can rip out that old thinking and replace it with new right thinking, we will look or feel completely different. The process is not easy and can be messy; we can feel like we are treading water, but renovating is so worth the trouble.

In the Bible there is a term called strongholds. The word *stronghold* means "fortress." In the Old Testament, a stronghold was a fortified dwelling used as a means of protection from an enemy. These physical structures, usually in caves high on a mountainside, were very difficult to assault. But think about our false beliefs as strongholds in our thinking. These fortresses are sending a message that affects what we do, what we say and are difficult to defeat.

Two primary areas will be attacked when it comes to false beliefs. The first will affect us and our identity, and the second will affect God and how we view Him. Having wrong thinking in either of these areas will create insecurity and instability.

What Do We Do With These Strongholds?

First, we must identify our false beliefs. If we cannot, then we cannot break free from them. The following are a few false beliefs.

- "I must please other people to be loved or accepted."
- "I am unworthy of love and acceptance."
- "I must have respect to know I have value."
- "I do not measure up."
- "In order to feel worthy, I must not fail."
- "Others cannot be trusted."
- "I do not need to change, or I will never change."

- "If I'm vulnerable, I will get hurt."
- "I don't need anyone."
- "My value is in my appearance."

[A more complete list can be found in the *Freedom Workbook*.]

Once we can identify the false belief, then we need to cast it out or get rid of it. We start by saying out loud, "I do not believe that I don't measure up, I do not believe that I will never change, I do not believe that my value comes from my appearance." I really believe that it's essential that we verbalize the false belief. There is power in what we speak and say. After we have spoken our false beliefs, we need to move into the last step which is extremely important. We need to replace the false belief with the truth. This step is so critical because if we do not replace the false belief with the truth, then the false belief will remain.

One of my false beliefs was "I must have respect to know I have value." What is the real truth? Genuine respect, honor, and value comes from God. Another one of my false beliefs was "I must perform or achieve to be accepted." The truth is, God accepts me just as I am not because of what I do. When my life is driven by this false belief, I continually feel insecure in who I am. When I believe the truth, I become confident in who I am, and I do not look for other people's approval or respect. Again, we need to speak the truth out loud. I don't want to make this sound too simple because it's not. Our goal is to create a new belief which takes time and consistency. We need to speak the truth daily until the truth becomes our new belief.

When we can begin to identify, cast out, and replace the false beliefs that have been controlling us, then we will experience real growth. This action step is connected to the next.

Action 2—Embrace Your Identity

When you first meet someone, the question that is often asked is "What do you do?" We are known by what we do. I love to play golf, and when I go to the golf course, I will play with whoever is available. Within the first couple of holes, I will get that question: "What do you do?" Sometimes I will "toy" with the person and say, "I am a consultant."

"What kind of consulting do you do?"

"Finding eternal life!"

When I first went into full-time ministry, I had a difficult time being called a pastor. For many years I was known as the operations manager for a company. I felt confident in what I did. But changing my occupation to me meant that I was changing my identity, so it was uncomfortable to say, "I am a pastor."

The problem with identifying ourselves with our professions or what we do: it gives us a wrong view of our identity. If our identity is based on what we do, then what happens when we do it no longer? Study after study shows that people who retire early live a shorter life. Why? There are differences of opinions, but for some reason, it just does. Could it be that when we don't have a purpose in life, we give up years of our life? The way that we think about our identity matters, it must not be tied to what we do; rather, our identity needs to be found in who we are.

When I addressed the subject of our false beliefs, I stated that we will be attacked in two areas: our view of God and our view of ourselves. Both are critical to experiencing positive change. How we view ourselves will literally affect everything we do and say. If I believe that my life doesn't matter, then I am worthless, I don't care about myself, I won't be motivated, my attitude will be negative, and most likely, I won't believe I can change. When we have an incorrect view of ourselves, we can cycle down into depression and hopelessness.

The opposite is also true. If I know who I am, I will have confidence, I will take risks, I will positively speak about myself and others, and most likely I will want to change. Finding our true identity will help us grow and move toward freedom.

And so, who are we? That identity must begin with where we came from. If we crawled out of the mud one day and evolved into a human being over millions of years, then our identity is a bit muddy. But if we were given life by the Creator God, then we find our identity and purpose through Him and not by chance. We will discover that we were not an accident, but we were given life for a reason. Jeremiah 29:11 says, *"For I know the plans I have for you," declares the* LORD, *"plans to prosper you and not to harm you, plans to give you hope and a future."* What truth is prominent in this verse to you? For me, this passage says that God knows me and has plans for me. The verse also tells me that every one of us has a purpose and that we are not an accident. He wants us to prosper, He wants to protect us, and He desires for us to have a future. For me, it brings hope.

Having a correct understanding of our identity must come from a proper understanding of God. We can develop our image of God in many ways. We hear thoughts from others, we read points of view about Him in books or on the Internet, and we form our decision on who He is. However, having the wrong concept of God will affect us in many ways, including questions about our self-worth, wondering about our purpose in life, and having uncertainty about our future. Having the right view of God is critical in our walk with God.

The more that we understand who God is, the more that we understand who we are. At this point is where we must start when we talk about finding our true identity. Examine how King David describes our relationship with God:

O Lord, you have examined my heart and know everything about me. You know when I sit down or stand up. You know my thoughts even when I'm far away. You see me when I travel and when I rest at home. You know everything I do. You know what I am going to say even before I say it, Lord.
(Psalm 139:1-4)

Have you ever considered the fact that God thinks about you? And He not only thinks about you, but He knows everything about you? At this very moment, as you read this book, God is watching you. I get so busy with life that I rarely even consider that thought. But knowing that God is concerned about every detail of my life changes my view of Him. I see how much He cares about me. If we are looking for our identity and wondering, *who am I?* We must understand that no one knows us like the One who gave us life—not our spouse or our best friend or even ourselves.

My struggle to find my identity for many years affected both my self-worth and my confidence. I tried to find my identity in my job, in the things I acquired, in the people I knew, and even in all that I learned, but my search left me empty. My view didn't change until I started to learn about God and how He viewed me; only then was I able to move forward.

So many voices tell us who we should be or who we shouldn't be. I watched a video documentary about college students being asked about the difference between men and women. Nearly every one of them ultimately said that there is no difference; "We can be whoever we want to be." This philosophy only brings confusion and insecurity.

Imagine for a minute that I was the creator of the smartphone. I developed the technology and put it all together. Of course, I would know everything about it—its capabilities, its limitations, and its maintenance. I would be the authority when it came to the smartphone.

Imagine for a moment that God created you. He knows every detail about your life. He knows your purpose, your abilities, and your limitations. He even knows how to help you and heal you in times of confusion or when you are at a loss. Wouldn't it make sense to ask Him who we are? One of my favorite verses in the Bible talks about our identity. Ephesians 2:10 says, *"For we are God's masterpiece. He has created us anew in Christ Jesus so we can do the good things he planned for us long ago."*

The word *masterpiece* means "a one-of-a-kind piece of art." You and I are God's masterpiece. He created us and gave us a new life. Some of us have felt like we are a mistake, but this verse assures us that we are definitely not. Every single person on this earth was given life and purpose by the God who is the Life giver. When we can embrace our identity, we are well on our way to freedom. Take a moment and thank God for who He has created you to be. Not one other person in all of life is like you. You are a one-of-a-kind piece of art.

Action 3—Identify and Replace

When I moved to Albuquerque, I immediately fell in love with the weather. Nearly every day was sunny, which was a stark difference from the Pacific Northwest. I had bought a bike in Portland the year before we moved, and I was looking forward to spending time peddling around the city. I did find a couple of obstacles to my biking, one being the wind. I moved at the end of April, and I quickly discovered that springtime is the "windy season" in New Mexico.

A few times when I was riding my bike, I was sailing along the path feeling good—until I had to turn around and ride back against the wind. I felt like someone was trying to hold me back from making progress. I quickly learned to look at my weather app before I decided to ride.

The other obstacle was coming in contact with goat heads—no, not a real goat's head but a piercing thorn that comes from a plant that is plentiful in the Southwest. These goat heads have multiple sharp thorns coming out in every direction. These vicious plants are not a welcome friend to bikers. After talking to some biking professionals, I decided to purchase different tires and tubes for my bike.

Changing your tube on the side of a road because of a collision with a goat head is no fun.

Changing a tire may not difficult but what about changing a bad habit or a character defect? The longer we have something the harder it is to change. All of us have bad habits but just in case you can't think of any, I looked up some of the most annoying habits that people possess.

- Biting your nails
- Picking your nose
- Spitting
- Fidgeting
- Making noise while eating
- Talking loudly on your phone
- Cracking your knuckles
- Standing in the middle of the sidewalk or aisle because you have an important text to respond to
- Belching
- Taking selfies

Did you see any that you identified with? When I was a young boy, I chewed my fingernails. I don't really know how or why it first started, but I would chew my nails down to where there was no more left to chew. My mother saw this bad habit that I had learned, and she decided to do something about it. She would paint my fingernails with a horrible tasting liquid designed to stop me from biting them. No matter how bad it tasted, I would eventually lick it or wash it off and continue chewing. I was messed up.

I don't remember how old I was, but something happened that would motivate me to change. It involved some of my classmates, namely girls seeing my fingernails. If you have ever seen someone that chews their nails, then you know it's not the most pleasing thing to view. I decided that for my own benefit, I needed to do something. I believe that within a few months of being intentional, my nail-biting days were over.

Changing a bad habit or a character defect is not easy. When I was younger and worked in the warehouse, we had a designated area that contained all of the items that had some sort of defect. Usually, a yellow slip was attached to the item, detailing what was wrong with the item. Eventually, we sorted each item with the vendor, and either shipped them back or disposed of them. Recognizing defects in our own lives does not mean that we should be disposed of—like machinery parts. Rather, we need to replace the defect—that flaw, weakness, or shortcoming—with something good. The Bible addresses "defects" in several places. I listed a couple of verses to give you an idea.

Get rid of all bitterness, rage, anger, harsh words, and slander, as well as all types of evil behavior. (Ephesians 4:31)

Put to death, therefore, whatever belongs to your earthly nature: sexual immorality, impurity, lust, evil desires and greed, which is idolatry. (Colossians 3:5)

First we have to identify and admit that what we are doing is not positive or healthy. One way that we can do this is by reading the bible. What does God want us to do and what character does He want us to exhibit? None of us are perfect; if we were, then we wouldn't need to change anything. Since we are not perfect, we need to work on changing our lives continually. The truth is, we will all change, but how we change is up to us. Whenever God tells us to do something, it is for our benefit. When He says to get rid of certain things, then we need to get rid of them. When He tells us to pursue certain things, then we need to pursue them.

Instead, be kind to each other, tenderhearted, forgiving one another, just as God through Christ has forgiven you. (Ephesians 4:32)

Since God chose you to be the holy people he loves, you must clothe yourselves with tenderhearted mercy, kindness, humility, gentleness, and patience. (Colossians 3:12)

When I was working in the warehouse years ago, I must admit that my language was not clean. I didn't even realize how bad my mouth had evolved in my teenage years. Once I started going to church, I quickly noticed that some of the words I routinely used were not appropriate. When I eventually surrendered to Christ, I knew that the time had come to clean up my language.

The process of replacing my "defective" word choice is similar to dispelling our false beliefs. We identify our defects, and then we replace them with positive or godly characteristics. When it comes to the words that we use, we take control of them. We simply have to choose to use self-control in our talk.

Our words have the power to change the course of our lives as well as the course of someone else's life. The Bible contains more than one verse that addresses our words.

"Do not let any unwholesome talk come out of your mouths, but only what helps build others up according to their needs, that it may benefit those who listen" (Ephesians 4:29).

This verse clearly states that whatever comes out of our mouth needs to be helpful, encouraging, and beneficial. This is what we need to strive for in our speech, and the good news is we don't have to do it on our own; we can ask for God's help. Always remember that God wants to help us change for the better. He is more than willing to assist us when it comes to replacing those things which are damaging to us as well as others. What has helped me in the past is whenever I identify something that I need to change, I pray and ask God to help me have self-control and to be aware of what I say.

Another common area is judging others. The first two churches I was involved with were very legalistic meaning everything was about rules. Women had to wear dresses, men had to be in a shirt and tie. There was no dancing or listening to certain music. The list went on and on. Legalism can create judgment of others. We feel superior because we are doing all of the right things, and they are less than because of the choices they are making. It took me many years to discover how wrong I had been. It is not my role to make sure people are living a certain way, it's God's role. Jesus said, do not judge or you will be judged. God has helped me replace my judgment of others with love and grace. Instead of judging others by their appearance or behavior, I have learned to remind myself that we all fall short. God loves every person the same.

Every one of us has defects in our lives. We are all a work in progress, but if we are intentional and are not satisfied with where we are, then we can work on change. Healthy change can bring freedom. The *Freedom* workbook contains helpful tools to guide you through this process.

Action 4—Practice Integrity

"What would you be willing to do for $10 million?" was the question asked of Americans in 1991. Two-thirds of those who were polled said that they would agree with at least one answer.

- Would abandon their entire family (25%)
- Would abandon their church (25%)
- Would become prostitutes for a week or more (23%)
- Would give up their American citizenship (16%)
- Would leave their spouse (16%)
- Would withhold testimony and let a murderer go free (10%)
- Would kill a stranger (7%)
- Would put up their children for adoption (3%)

I was shocked when I read these choices and the results, but I can't help but think, *what would people agree to today?* Have we moved forward in our values or have we slipped backward? When we look at the choice to grow, we must look at the trait of integrity—doing what you say you will do, keeping your word, letting your "yes" be "yes" and your "no" be "no." Integrity is being honest, choosing not to compromise, *having* godly character not *being* a character. The best way to learn about character is by studying the Bible.

In Genesis, a man named Jacob had twelve sons. One of his sons named Joseph was Jacob's favorite. The other brothers were so jealous of Joseph they didn't need a reason to dislike their younger brother. Joseph had a dream that he shared with his brothers. "One day," he said, "All of you will bow before me." Can you imagine how his brothers took the news?

The dream was the final straw. Several of his brothers spoke of killing him, but instead, they sold him to some slave traders. Talk about dysfunctional family! He was taken to Egypt where he was sold to Potiphar, a man of influence and captain of the guard for Pharaoh. As a slave, Joseph was faithful in everything that he did and was given charge over Potiphar's entire household. As a rule, when everything seems to be going well, temptation often rears its ugly head.

Such was true in Joseph's life. Handsome young men are seldom overlooked, and Potiphar's wife noticed him. She repeatedly tried to entice Joseph into her bedroom. He repeatedly refused her offers. She continued to persist, and Joseph refused.

"Look," he told her, "my master trusts me with everything in his entire household. ⁹No one here has more authority than I do. He has held back nothing from me except you, because you are his wife. How

could I do such a wicked thing? It would be a great sin against God." (Genesis 39:8-9)

Notice that Joseph did not say that he would be sinning against her husband but against God. Remembering whatever we do will affect God is important. Why? Because God wants the best for us, and He doesn't want us to get hurt.

One day when no one was around but Joseph and Potiphar's wife, she caught hold of him in an attempt to entice him to the bedroom. At this point, Joseph's level of integrity was about to be tested.

If we know that what we do will never be found out by others, what will we do? Integrity is choosing to do the right thing whether or not someone is watching or whether they find out. Whatever you and I battle, we will have the same test that Joseph had. People are tempted to look at pornography on their computers or phone, knowing that no one will ever know. What could be the harm of only a look?! The same is true of food, pills, drinking, smoking, and so forth. Our decisions and the choices that we make will reveal what's important to us and what we value. Will we value pleasure, selfishness, and desire, or will we value our character?

What choice would Joseph make? He pulled away from her and *ran* out of the house, leaving a garment in her hands. His was definitely the right decision. I would love to say that Joseph lived a peaceful, joyful life, knowing that he made the right choice. Potiphar's wife screams for her servants, turns around the truth, and says that Joseph was trying to have his way with her. When Potiphar returned and heard her story, he was outraged and gave orders to throw Joseph into prison. What happened to Joseph seems so unfair, doesn't it? Joseph made the right decision and possessed integrity, yet he suffered the consequences. Joseph had a new home in a dark, cold jail cell.

We can only imagine what thoughts were running through his mind during those next couple of years. God always honors those who possess integrity, and Joseph was elevated from the prison to the second in command in the entire country of Egypt, thereby saving thousands of lives. All of the details of Joseph's story can be found in Genesis chapters 39 to 42.

Each day our integrity will be tested. Years ago, I was helping a salesman who was picking up some packages. When he went inside to talk with the owner of our company, I grabbed the boxes and took them to his car that was parked out on the street. When I placed the boxes on his trunk, I hit his electric antennae and snapped it off. Did I mention that he was driving a Mercedes-Benz? I couldn't believe what I had inadvertently done.

When he came out to his car, he asked, "Did you load the boxes?"

I replied, "Yes." During that brief interchange, I had a choice to reveal what I had done. I said nothing and failed the test of integrity.

A few weeks later, the salesman stopped by and mentioned that someone had broken off his antenna.

I listened to him, knowing that replacing that antenna would likely cost a good amount of money. I said nothing and completely failed the test of integrity again.

Why do we choose to do exactly what we know is wrong? In my case, fear kept me from admitting the accident. I was afraid of getting in trouble with the company. I have already addressed the subject of fear and how being fearful can literally stop or paralyze us. Fear is a powerful emotion. We fail to come clean after we lie because of fear. We don't admit that we drank or used drugs because of fear. We fail to tell about our decision to gamble at the casino because of fear. When we try to avoid the consequences, we are systematically compromising our character.

Little things generally turn into bigger things. We don't tell the whole truth, we take a few items from work, or we hide a text message from our spouse. Every relationship hinges on integrity. If you discover that a friend has been lying to you or spreading gossip about you, then the friendship will most likely end. In a marriage, if one spouse learns the other is hiding something from him or her, the relationship will suffer because of the lack of integrity.

Regardless of what we have done in our past, the good news is we can choose to change today!

Practical Steps That Will Help Build Your Character

- When you tell someone that you will do something, follow through.
- When you are given responsibility, do your very best.
- Always be honest and speak the truth.
- Take ownership of your words and actions.

As you choose to make integrity a core value in your life, you will see the growth as well as the positive results that come with that decision.

Action 5—Relapse Prevention

The year was 2006. Kathy and I had begun to see some changes in our oldest daughter that deeply concerned us. Every parent hopes for the best and tries to justify when their child goes through a difficult season, and our daughter was having one of those difficult seasons. Little did we know how difficult her situation would prove to be. She had been involved in a serious relationship a couple of years earlier that ended in heartbreak. This loss in her life started a dark road that would not conclude for several years.

When she was young, we were fortunate to provide her a Christian education until her final years of high school. We decided to move her into a public school so that she would have greater opportunities leading up to graduation. Ours seemed like a good plan at the time; our desire was for her to have a reliable and safe education. We didn't realize that regardless of where you place your child in school, temptations always arise. During her teenage years in that private Christian school, we did not know that she would be introduced to drugs. Simply because the institution advertises "private" and "Christian" does not mean that the school will be without problems. Drugs are no respecter of a person, religion or status. Unfortunately, kids are introduced to recreational drugs at a young age well before they have an understanding of the real dangers.

When our daughter finished school, she continued to struggle off and on for the next several years. Not until 2006 did we know something was seriously wrong. Even though there are sure signs that showed the evidence of addiction, at the time we never knew or understood what those clues looked like. Kathy and I made one of the hardest decisions that we have ever had to make. We told our daughter that she needed to leave our home. We had the safety of our other children to consider, and our oldest daughter's behavior was becoming a problem for them.

Soon after we made this difficult decision, we discovered the real problem—heroin addiction. I believe both Kathy and I were in shock and denial when we finally learned the reason for her erratic behavior. We were haunted by the question: *How could our daughter be addicted to heroin?* We had raised her in a Christian home, she attended church every week, she knew right from wrong, and drugs were definitely wrong. My mind screamed, *there has to be a mistake!* Only no mistake had been made. When we cleaned out her room after she left, we found items that work very efficiently when shooting heroin. Spoons and cotton balls scattered all over the floor.

Our daughter moved in with her sister who had just married, and life became steadily worse. Both of our daughters were now using, and our granddaughter was right in the middle of it. During this season of life, our family felt like it was being ripped apart. Addiction doesn't only affect the addict; it affects the entire family. Those years seemed more like a nightmare than reality. The daily struggle seemed hopeless.

Years went by, and eventually, our daughter agreed to get help. We called a 30-day inpatient facility in our city, and we were excited to find out that there was a bed available. We dropped off our daughter, and the first step that she faced was detoxing. We had absolutely no idea about the battle our daughter was facing, and detoxing would prove to be one of her most difficult challenges. Heroin does not give up its hold easily, and the body feels like it is fighting for its life as the heroin leaves the system. She finally finished the program, and we had hope that we could begin to move forward, but we were wrong. She relapsed. We all had much more to learn about addiction.

As studies continue on addiction, researchers are discovering that a relapse is not merely a singular event but multiple setbacks along the road to recovery. Our daughter would relapse twice more before experiencing freedom. The reasons for relapse and their prevention is what I want to tackle in this action step.

I asked my daughter why she thought she had relapsed, and she said there were a few different reasons. One was the fact that she first went into treatment because other people wanted her to go. Committing herself wasn't her decision; she only tried because it *felt* right to do. The other reason was the people who surrounded her. One of the treatment centers that she went into was Christ-centered. We talked with the directors, and our daughter was accepted into the program.

We were really excited. When she began, the program looked very promising, giving her structure, responsibility, and dignity. The facility was set up with a couple of houses that the girls would live in. They attended different meetings each day and learned life principles. About two months had passed when a girl came into the program and joined our daughter in the house. Little did we know that things were about to change. A few days went by, and we received a call and found out that our daughter was being expelled from the program for using.

Everything had looked so positive; we couldn't understand what had happened. We later found out that the girl who joined our daughter's house had been brought in by her grandparents, and they were desperate to get her help. She wasn't there for the right reasons, so she brought drugs into the house with her. Temptation plus opportunity equals relapse.

Whatever you are struggling with, there will be the possibility of relapse. The good news is that we can be aware of predictable signs to help prevent relapse. Each of these signs has indicators that give us a warning. Knowing these signs is like seeing the "check engine light" come on in your car. The light warns of a potential problem. If you do nothing about that warning, then it will likely lead to a costly problem. The signs I will share are somewhat similar. Each of these stages are sending us a message.

Losing Focus

During this stage the person pulls away from others and what keeps him or her on the right path. He or she fails to follow through with commitments, stops attending support groups, hides the truth, and becomes overconfident, believing that their struggle is over. Their personal time with God becomes inconsistent and less critical.

The same can also happen when we become involved in a relationship. The focus is placed on someone else instead of our recovery; our energy is now centered on them. We shift our priorities away from the things that we need in order to stay healthy. We need to ask ourselves, "Which of these actions do I fall into?" The goal of relapse prevention is knowing our personal patterns and sharing them with our accountability partner. When someone else is aware of our weaknesses then they can help us stay on the right path.

Chaos

This stage occurs when something happens that we were not prepared for, such as conflict arising in our marriage or with our children, financial pressure, or the death of a loved one. We feel the pressures of life closing in on us, we are overwhelmed, and we have negative thoughts or fear that can consume us. We try to outrun our thoughts by working more, exercising, skipping meals or binge eating. We do not want to be around people or talk with them on a deeper level. Slowing down or relaxing can seem unreachable goals. Facing chaos can cause us to judge, be critical and gossip about others in an effort to avoid our own issues. Chaos can affect our concentration, sleep, and our decision-making ability. When life gets chaotic, our thinking becomes distorted, and relapse is getting closer. Ask yourself, "what actions do I turn to during stressful times"? If we can be aware of our tendencies and share them with another person, we can prevent relapse from happening.

Emotional Imbalance

When we lose our focus and life become chaotic, the pressure can cause us to overreact, become defensive, argue, and be angry. Our emotions tend to drive our actions. Because we have pulled away from others, we feel alone. Therefore, we try to manage life on our own. We can have highs and lows in our emotions, we can lash out at others, or we can turn inward and feel the turmoil inside of us, which can affect us physically with things like stomach issues and headaches. Our body is telling us that we are losing control. Again, we need to be honest with ourselves and others by acknowledging which of these actions we turn to. You can see why it's so important to have another person helping you. Emotional imbalance is telling us that relapse is knocking on our door.

Burnout

This is the final stage before relapse. Most of us understand burnout because we have been there with little-to-no energy, the feeling of hopelessness or depression. It becomes difficult for us to think; our physical weariness makes concentration extremely difficult. When we reach this place, our thoughts begin to focus on our coping behavior. At this point we think about old friends or going to places where we shouldn't be going.

I heard about a man who had been clean from sexual addiction for some time, and he was driving somewhere on an errand. He saw a young woman who was hitchhiking and decided to pull over to give her a ride, believing he was only trying to help someone. On the inside, he was thinking of something completely different. The temptation and the opportunity had presented themselves, and he relapsed. That one decision he made would have serious consequences.

I maintain that this decision didn't just happen when he picked up a hitchhiker; that decision evolved over time. The limbic system of our brain, which is wired to send messages of survival, knows what will take away our pain and replace it with pleasure. Without our consciously knowing or understanding, we end up doing what we don't want to do.

These four different stages build upon each other, starting with losing focus, then chaos happens, and because we feel overwhelmed, we soon end up in emotional imbalance. Our emotions fluctuate, and we eventually burnout, which inevitably will lead to relapse. Ask yourself this question: "What does relapse look like for me?" Our workbook teaches the reader how to identify these actions which will, in turn, help prevent relapse. An essential part of this action step is sharing your personal indicators with another person. It is nearly impossible to hold ourselves accountable and to see when we slide towards relapse.

Being healthy is the opposite of relapse. The key is to stay focused on what is essential. We do this by going to meetings, keeping our commitments, staying humble, reaching out to others instead of isolating, and making God a priority in your life.

After making the choice to grow comes the final choice to make.

Chapter 5
THE CHOICE TO CONNECT

D o you know what a flock of quail is called? This is an excellent question for a crossword puzzle. The answer is a *covey*. Quail are social animals that travel in a covey so that they can spot any enemy that would like to have them for lunch. In fact, they even roost in a circular formation so that one of them can spot any approaching danger. Humans can learn several lessons from the quail. They have learned that being alone can be a very dangerous place to be.

I read in a *Fortune* magazine that half of the American people feel lonely. Do you ever feel lonely or isolated and have no one with whom to talk or with whom to share your life? In a recent survey taken by Cigna, a healthcare company, the age group most prone to loneliness were those born between the mid-'90s and the early 2000s or what is known as the "Z" generation. The study also learned that 46 percent of Americans report feeling lonely sometimes or always. Out of the 20,000 people who were surveyed, only about half (53 percent, to be exact) report having meaningful, in-person social interactions with friends or family on a daily basis.

What is happening in our society? We are seemingly becoming more and more isolated. Could it be that connecting via social media has replaced the personal one-on-one interaction?

When I moved from the state of Washington to New Mexico, I spent six weeks by myself and away from my family. I tried to keep myself occupied, but I really didn't know anyone. My entire family, friends and support system were some 1400 miles away. Each day after I got home from work, I tried to keep myself busy with physical activity. I would ride my bike, go for a walk or play a little golf. Unfortunately, I found that physical activity was no replacement for personal connection. Studies have indicated that loneliness affects our physical health, increasing our stress which can lead to depression, heart problems, and other issues. Too often when people feel isolated and depressed, they are given prescription drugs to help deal with the issues of life. But think about that solution: are we only dealing with the symptoms instead of the root causes?

From the very beginning, man was created for community and connection. Genesis 2:18b says, *"It is not good for the man to be alone...."* I don't know about you, but I would definitely say that being alone is not good for me.

When I looked up the definition of *loneliness,* I was somewhat surprised at my findings. The dictionary said, "being without company or friends, cut off from others and sad from being alone and having no one with whom to talk." Even the dictionary supports what many surveys have found. Being alone is not good for us. Now there is a difference between loneliness and wanting to have time alone. Moments when we can get away can be healthy for us.

Everyone has a favorite place to be alone. Some like to go for a drive, some like to read a book, some curl up in bed and watch a good movie, but for me personally, I love going out in nature. As I write this chapter, I am sitting outside in a lounge chair, listening to the birds singing and looking at the mountains in Tucson, Arizona. Spending time alone has some great benefits from helping us unwind and decompress from the pressures of life to thinking better. When we can take away all of the distractions of life, we can concentrate better, which helps us make wiser decisions.

Having times of being alone is different than wanting to be alone constantly. If you dislike people and your greatest desire is to move to a remote area of Alaska, then something is wrong with you. Usually, that decision involves people, and more specifically, being hurt by people. When we have been hurt by others and our trust has been broken, then why would we want to be around anyone? The answer is that we wouldn't, but we need to put aside those feelings. We need others for multiple reasons, which I will address in the action steps throughout this chapter.

Consider the message of Genesis 2:18b, *"It is not good for the man to be alone...."* Why would God make such a statement? He said it because it was the truth; He created us to need companionship. He said it because being alone is not His desire or His plan. You and I are made for connection. If we weren't, then God would have stopped when He created Adam.

The following action steps will show how connection can and will make a difference in our lives.

Action 1—Connect with God

When I first met Kathy, I was attracted to her because she was beautiful. Though I had an instant attraction to her, I really did not know her. Whenever we meet someone for the first time, we are likely meeting the best version of that person. When we don't really know the other person, we feel somewhat insecure. We smile, say nice things, talk about the weather and other superficial matters. What we are doing is trying to determine whether this person is safe. What is the gauge for feeling safe? I think that it only can happen after spending time with the other person.

When Kathy and I first met, we seemed to have so much in common, but as time passed and we let down our guard, things became much more difficult. The months leading up to our marriage were somewhat rocky. One of us would make an off-the-cuff unkind or thoughtless comment, and instantly we would be in a fight. How you fight will determine your future together. We didn't know how to fight because we were both so broken. What held us together was our love for each other and our love for God, without those two things we wouldn't have made it.

I well remember our wedding day; it played out like a bad dream. Yes, you did read that correctly. We had a lovely ceremony and reception after which everything turned to the dark side. My goal of being a man was to leave immediately for our honeymoon. I had reserved a room at a motel in Medford, Oregon, to spend our first night together. Then we planned to drive to Southern California and spend the week together experiencing Disneyland and other exciting places.

My wife's mother had her own plans and agenda, which is where the tension started. She wanted us to come over and spend the entire evening with all of the relatives

I didn't know. After a brief conflict, we went over to her house and spent some time with my new family. After a couple of hours, it was definitely time to go. We said our goodbyes, but my new mother-in-law wasn't happy.

The situation was already tense, but then I made an even bigger mistake. I blamed my wife for the change of plans. We ended up in a fight for the next four hours as we drove to the motel. What a great start to our new life ahead!

How did we make it through difficult times like this? I believe it was our love and a multitude of prayers. Love is often expressed as a feeling that we have, but actually love is a commitment. If we do not have the right understanding of love, then love can come and go like every other emotion. Our love for each other and our love for God has been the reason that we have been married for over thirty years.

The most important relationship that we can have in life is with God. It's not simply a matter of knowing who God is; it's doing life together with Him. When you think about building a relationship, I would have to say that the most important element is trust. You must have trust in the other person if you plan to move forward together. If trust isn't involved, then you will continuously be insecure with the person, and the relationship will suffer. The same is true with God. I believe the trust issue is one of the primary reasons why people push God aside. They do not trust God. But trust comes through experience—exactly like it has in my marriage. Trust doesn't simply happen; it is built over the passage of time.

From time to time, I meet with a couple who are going through the pain of an affair. Sometimes the couple agrees to work on repairing the marriage. Even though making needed adjustments seems impossible, it's not. The most challenging part of healing revolves around trust. The intimate relationship the couple once shared was virtually nonexistent because the trust had been broken. Can this marriage be saved? Yes…but it will take time and honesty. With honesty and trust comes an element of risk. If I am honest and if I trust you, then I can be hurt by you. However, if I am not honest and if I don't trust you, then we cannot move forward.

The book of Proverbs was written by King Solomon, the wisest man who ever walked on this earth outside of Jesus. He wrote in the third chapter that we should trust the Lord with all of our heart and not lean on our own understanding. Why? The *Merriam-Webster Dictionary* defines *trust* as "the assured reliance on the character, ability, strength, or truth of someone." Do you view God in this way?

In whatever area we struggle, we need someone who is completely reliable and trustworthy on our side. We need someone who understands what we are facing and can help us with unlimited resources. I have only found one person with those kind of credentials, and I want to build a relationship with Him. The following are ways we can build that relationship.

First of all, we need to spend time with God daily. Spending time with Him is not a one-and-done thing that happens in the morning or before you go to bed. We spend time with Him throughout our day. No healthy relationship talks for a brief time in the morning or the evening and then is silent for the rest of the day. Relating to someone is continual. We learn to ask Him for wisdom when making a decision or when seeking to help another person. Building a relationship is having a grateful heart and thanking Him for all that He provides for us daily. We make a habit of connection with Him.

Prayer is communicating with God. In 1 Thessalonians 5:17, the Bible commands us to pray without ceasing. What a great goal when it comes to connecting with God.

Secondly, we need to spend time reading the Bible each day. The Bible is our life instruction manual that tells us how to live, what to do and what to stay away from. I have found writing down something that God is showing me after I read is helpful. Some call this the practice of journaling. I must admit that I have been inconsistent over the years in this area, but when I do follow through, it helps me retain so much more.

Many people ask where to start when reading the Bible. Sixty-six books have been written by 40 different authors over a period of 1500 years. Reading the Word of

God can seem a daunting task. I usually tell people to start by reading the book of John, which was written by one of the disciples who walked with Jesus. He shares a great picture of who Jesus is.

If you want to read through the entire Bible, then I would suggest getting a reading plan. Several of them can be found on the web. One word of caution: more is not always better. Read at a comfortable pace and ask yourself questions: who wrote the book, to whom the book was written, what the context of the message is, and what you can take away or apply to your life. If you find that you don't understand something, write it down and ask your accountability partner or a pastor.

Listening also helps in building our relationship with God. Listening seems to be a lost art. People are always ready to talk or to reply, but listening forces us to pause and take note. Years ago, I attended a conference that included a break-out session on listening. I went with a couple of leaders from our church, and we decided to go to the session on listening. The speaker said, "Turn to the person next to you." (My comfort was the guy with whom I came who was sitting next to me.) I turned to him. She said, "Look into the person's eyes for two minutes and then ask God what He wanted to say to that person."

Wow! Looking into someone's eyes for two minutes is a long time and is uncomfortable! Try it with someone to see how difficult it is.

The first minute I didn't hear anything, and maybe that was the point. I had to focus and really listen to what God was saying. I finally heard God say that He loved this person and that He was proud of the man that he was. God's message actually touched me to the point of tears forming in my eyes. With that exercise, that speaker really proved to me that God wants to speak to each of us if we are available.

The first chapter addressed surrendering to Christ. This choice is crucial to our eternal life, but so is building our relationship with Him. Connecting with God doesn't just happen on its own; it takes action on our part.

Action 2—Connect with Others

Connecting with others is crucial when we walk through the freedom process. Because we cannot do it on our own, trying to do it on our own is what holds us back from change. We will always have the temptation to believe that if we can work harder, and if we set our mind to it, then we can change. Unfortunately, it just doesn't work; we need others.

Let me make a disclaimer: we need others, but we need the right kind of others. When you consider your life and those relationships that you have had, who influences you the most? The closer someone is to you, the more that person can change you. That person can also be your greatest asset or your greatest deterrent. Recognizing the difference between healthy and unhealthy people is vital to relationships. The difference may seem obvious, but it really isn't. We are all attracted to certain types of people. Oftentimes we choose them because of our own needs or insecurities. For example, if you don't feel loved or you have a poor self-image, you may be drawn to someone who takes an interest in you or speaks some flattering words without knowing who the person really is. In a sense, we can be blinded. We move into a relationship with someone who is unhealthy and then wonder what happened. How can we know that someone is healthy or unhealthy?

Characteristics of Unhealthy or Toxic People

These individuals can use us, hurt us and bring us down. Sometimes we don't even recognize how unhealthy the other person is until the relationship evolves into an abusive one. The reason this happens points back to our own unmet needs. We are looking for a person to meet a need in us that they cannot meet.

Perhaps you know someone who is controlling. Often a controlling person looks good on the outside, and they say all the things that we need to hear. They can come across as confident and put together, but they wear only a façade. We fall for it because we are looking for acceptance and love. But controlling people want to know where you have been and what you've been doing. They can be overbearing, demanding and manipulative. If we connect with controlling people, the relationship will never end well.

How can we know if someone has a controlling personality? Take time in developing the relationship, set boundaries, and see how the person reacts. If the person becomes angry and aggressive, it's time to end the relationship or get help. Another indicator of being unhealthy or toxic is someone who is negative or critical. At first, the person acts normal and says all of the right things. We can be drawn to them because again, we are looking for someone who cares about us. With the passage of time, the words of controlling people change to negative and critical. They put others down because they don't feel good about who they are. They can be judgmental or continuously complaining. Controlling people always express what they don't like or what they disapprove of. Nothing is ever good enough. Again, take your time moving forward in the relationship and set healthy boundaries by saying, "I don't think that we need to put down others," or "I don't like what you are saying about me." How they respond will show you who they are.

If you find that you choose toxic or unhealthy people, then seek input from someone whom you trust and respect. Let them help you see the situation more clearly.

One of the most significant problems that can come from unhealthy, toxic people is that they are not supportive, encouraging nor interested in anyone but themselves. This is not the type of person that we need moving forward. So what does a healthy person look like? This is what I want to share with you. Some of us have never had a healthy relationship. In fact, as I go through some of the characteristics, ask yourself if you have anyone that meets these qualities.

Let's look at the five characteristics of a healthy person.

Five Characteristics of a Healthy Person

Supportive. Every person who is breathing needs support. If we are trying to make the right choices along with positive change, then we need someone who will support us. A supportive person is one who holds us up and believes in us. Someone who is supportive will listen to us and give positive feedback without putting us down. These people stay with us no matter what. Through their actions as well as their words, they show their support.

Encouraging. We all need real encouragement, which the Bible describes as building courage in someone or building another person's confidence. We need encouraging people in our lives. I have been blessed over the years to have several people encourage me. I first started singing because a person encouraged me, and I ended up leading worship in church for fifteen years. People encouraged me to start speaking, and I have been speaking for twenty years. When I thought about writing a book, a couple of people encouraged me to undertake the task. The result of their encouragement is this book you are reading. Encouragement helps us go beyond our comfort zone. What could you accomplish with encouragement?

Respect. The way that we talk to or treat the other person will indicate whether or not we respect them. When we respect someone, we speak to the person openly, and we listen to what he or she has to say. We honor their boundaries. We don't try to control someone or make them do what we want them to do. Respect allows the other person to have freedom. When we know that people respect us, we will be drawn to them because we know that they are for us.

Honesty. Of course, honesty is essential. We don't need someone in our life who is dishonest. Honesty is telling the truth instead of telling us what we would like to hear. Honesty is the ability to say the truth in a way that is not judgmental or condemning. An honest person is someone on whom we can depend. Knowing that another person is honest and for us gives us the confidence to move forward.

Trustworthy. Trust is definitely the glue that holds a relationship together. I already shared how important it is for God to be trustworthy but equally important is trust in others. When we can trust what someone says and what he does, then no questions will arise about their commitment. Trust means that the person is reliable and safe. Finding someone who is trustworthy will help us not only in our freedom but also in our healing.

These five characteristics are important when we are connecting with others. Pursuing a relationship like this may seem overwhelming, but so worth the investment. People are the primary reason for hurt and heartache, and people are what we need to be healed. Do you have anyone in your life who is healthy? If you don't, then I would encourage you to start by praying and asking God to bring someone into your life. We also must be proactive because the person most likely will not be searching for us. An excellent place to start looking is in a church or a community group. We need to put ourselves into different environments with people, even if it is difficult.

Action 3—Give Back to Others

Are you a safe person? I have asked myself that question many times. Sometimes I would say yes, and other times I would say no. As much as we need healthy safe people around us, we also need to be a healthy safe person for others. A safe person is supportive, encouraging and genuinely cares about others. Walking through the process of recovery goes both ways; we receive, but we must give as well.

When you are hurting or struggling in life, the focus becomes on you. This change of focus is not necessarily bad because you do need to focus on getting healthy. However, a time will come when we need to take the focus off of ourselves and focus on others. In fact, I believe that reaching out to others can bring us healing and health. The Bible says that if we give, it will be given back to us. The amount you give will determine the amount you receive. We cannot out-give God, and He wants us to give to one another because giving will not only help a needy person or benefit us, but it will please God. Studies show that giving brings benefits like reduced blood pressure, diminished stress and anxiety, and even an increased lifespan.

Now you may be saying, "I am not sure that I have anything to give to others." Listen carefully: we *all* have things to offer. Looking at certain people who are gifted and talented and thinking, *I am nothing like them* is easy. You are right; you are nothing like them, and you don't need to be like them. God has given us all unique gifts and talents. What you can give another person, I cannot provide. What I can give to someone, you cannot provide. This distinctiveness is what makes us unique and equally beneficial.

Some of us are encouragers, some love to help others, and some of us are good with money. Some are musical, some are organized, and some possess artistic ability. Some are teachers, some are mechanics, and some love to cook. What you love to do is what you can give to others.

I have had several opportunities in the past to give back to others. Let me share about a couple of these opportunities. Several years ago our church decided to be a blessing to some patients with a long-term illness at a convalescent home. Most of them could not walk without assistance or leave their rooms. When I first arrived, the odor of urine was so strong that I wasn't sure if I would be able to continue. I went to the first room, and the entrance was covered by a curtain. After I introduced myself, I realized that the lady wasn't able to talk coherently. I did not let her condition be a hindrance. I read a few verses from the Bible and shared a little about myself. She listened and nodded her head. Before I left, I said, "God loves you, and you are very special."

What did I give this dear lady? Kindness! We can all give kindness to others. For me, it was a great day to spend a few hours ministering to others in that convalescent home.

When I was in my late twenties, I was in a singing group with a few other people. We traveled to various venues to share our music. Several of the places that we would visit were places that rarely saw visitors. The best part was after our singing was over. That's when the people would come and talk to us as we listened to their stories. I look back on the times now and think, *our singing wasn't the greatest, but we were able to give these dear people a listening ear and kindness.*

Another time our church decided to help the homeless in Portland, Oregon. We piled into different vehicles and headed downtown. Five or six people from the church were riding in my car, and we drove around not quite knowing where we were going. After all, homeless folks do not have a physical address. We finally stopped when we saw some people who were apparently in need and started handing out lunches, socks, and coats. The people were taken back by our generosity because they didn't expect strangers to give them anything that time of night. I can assure you that we were the ones who were the most blessed.

I was talking to one of the men after church one Sunday, and he commented, "God has given so much to me, but I haven't given anything to God."

I immediately responded, "Oh, yes, you have!"

He looked at me with shock and surprise written all across his face.

I reminded him that before and after church he drove a golf cart taking people to and from their cars. "My friend, you are giving back to God by helping others!" He hadn't even thought about that service for others in respect to giving. Sometimes we feel that we have to do something really big to give to others, but God simply wants us to give what we have. Sometimes the simple things that make the most significant impact.

I believe that most of us have fallen into the fast-paced busyness of the world with little time to invest in others. How rare it is to see someone express kindness to a person. The opposite is often the norm. People are often rude, angry, and self-absorbed. We can make a difference if we choose to give back to others. When we do that, we are trading selfishness for selflessness. It's amazing how good we can feel when we give ourselves to others.

Action 4—Share Your Testimony

As you might imagine, losing our four-month-old son to sudden infant death syndrome (SIDS) was absolutely devastating to us. When we looked into the meaning of SIDS, we learned that it was an unexpected death of an infant less than a year old. This sterile meaning did not bring us any peace whatsoever. We had no details or explanation for his death. When parents lose a child, they don't simply move on and forget the past.

What bothered us the most was what had happened the day before he passed away. Kathy took him to the doctor to receive his scheduled immunizations. When she brought him home that day, he was increasingly fussy, and she could tell that he wasn't feeling well. We assumed his fussiness resulted from his shots. We figured he only needed a good rest that night. To our utter shock, that night of sleep would be his last.

My wife was diligent in searching for answers. She found a lawyer who heard about our tragedy and decided to take our case pro bono (without charge). Ours was the only pro-bono case that he chose to take for the entire year, and we were extremely thankful. He spent countless hours looking into all of the data and ultimately filed a suit against the federal government because all immunizations are protected by the government.

Kathy and I were notified that we would have to give testimony over the phone. The day came, and we were told that we were under oath. We were asked several questions, and we did our best to answer honestly. Several weeks passed before we heard the final decision; we lost the case because the coroner who did our son's autopsy completely mishandled the postmortem examination. Very little evidence remained to support our claim. Even though we lost the suit, we still felt we had discovered the reason for his death. Our attorney was 95 percent sure that the immunizations caused his death. The suit was never about the money for us; we only wanted answers.

The things in life that are the most painful are often our greatest asset. You might be wondering how that can possibly be true. A couple of years after the loss of our firstborn son, I decided to share my story at our church. I don't think I was ready for what was ahead. At the time we offered five services between Saturday and Sunday. Each time I shared about losing my son Justin, I broke down and cried. I had moments when I wasn't sure if I could continue my testimony. You would think that after sharing a couple of times, I wouldn't be quite as emotional, but you would be as wrong as I was.

What transpired after each service is what surprised me. Singles and couples came to me who had lost a child in the past. The pain is what connected us. What I learned that weekend was how important our story was. Sharing about Justin's loss wasn't something that I looked forward to telling others, but that story created a bond between myself and others who had a similar story. Knowing that someone understands what we have gone through creates a connection.

Everyone has a story. Maybe you have heard this phrase before, but it is true. No one in the world has the same story that you have. Think for a moment that every person that you pass by at the grocery store or the gas station or at the health club has something to share.

One of the things I really enjoy about being a pastor is all of the different people that I meet. On the outside, they may look like just an average person, but when you start listening to them, they have unique experiences that are both good and bad. Those experiences truly make us who we are. Much of our life has been molded by those different experiences and people along our journey. I can personally look back and see how certain events and certain people have steered my life to where it is today.

Whatever you are struggling with, there are many people just like you. In the group that I have led for several years, there are always people who come for the first time. I invite them to join me for a few minutes as I explain to them the different resources that we have. During that time, I tell them that one of the fears that people have when they come is that no one understands what they are facing. I often see people shaking their heads or connecting with me through their nonverbal expressions. Then I say, "But you are wrong. Every person here is struggling with something, and many are struggling with the same issue that you are."

Just to provide context, several hundred people attend. I tell the visitors that they are in the right place to find hope. Fear often keeps people from reaching out and getting the needed help. One of the "fear breakers" is when someone meets another person who has struggled with a same struggle. One man, who I will call John, attended my group and afterward told me that he was a member of a biker gang, and his life was falling apart. "My wife is leaving me, I'm involved in drugs, and I have done some horrible things," he confessed. I could see the hopelessness in his eyes.

I immediately said, "Stay where you are." I quickly went to our drummer and asked him to come talk to the man. Why? Because our drummer was once a member of a very bad biker gang. He had lived in the same lifestyle as this man who was faced with hopelessness. Our drummer understood the battle and could share his story of hope with him. Seeing the two of them connect as they shared with each other was amazing.

You also have a testimony—a unique story with unique experiences. Someone has said that without a test you can't have a testimony. Though we didn't see it at the time, when we lost our son Justin, God would use that test to become part of our testimony. As a Christ follower, our testimony is sharing how Jesus changed our lives and how God has helped us through those difficult tests in life.

When preparing your testimony, consider dividing your life into three segments. The first segment is what your life was like before Christ. For me, mine was hopeless, without any direction or any purpose, and I felt like I lived in survival mode. Basically, my life revolved around me and what I wanted, which created loneliness.

The next segment of your testimony is sharing how you came to a saving knowledge of Christ. I received an invitation to go to church with a friend, but what had been happening inside of me was the groundwork. Without even knowing it, I was searching for something that could fill the emptiness inside of me. This person came into my life and invited me to go to church. There I found the needed answers and a God who loved me.

The last segment of our testimony is sharing what has happened since we have asked Christ to come into our lives. This segment was huge for me as everything was in change mode—how I talked, what I desired, my relationships, and my life's purpose. Knowing Christ eventually led me into full-time ministry. Knowing Christ personally made the difference for Kathy and me after losing our son. Pain will either draw you closer to God or push you away from

Him. If we blame God, then we will distance ourselves from Him. If we trust God, then we will draw closer to Him because we need His help and His comfort. I have seen many people become bitter because they blame God, and tragically they end up all alone and depressed.

A couple of times a year, we schedule several people to share their testimony at our church gathering. I believe these times become some of our most valuable services. Why? Because people connect with personal stories of change. We tell each person or couple that they have between three and five minutes to share. That time allotment may seem like a very short time, but you would be surprised by the power of their short story.

You probably have noticed that much of my book contains stories about myself and others. I hope that these stories speak to you in some way. Jesus was the Master Storyteller. If you read through the first four books of the New Testament, you will find that Jesus used stories to teach others about life-changing principles.

As you share your story with someone, you may provide the key to unlock the person's pain. If you have never written out your testimony, take some time and break it down into three parts, keeping it short, and then share it with someone. You will never know the difference that you can make until you begin sharing.

CONCLUSION

Change is never easy. When we made the move from Washington to New Mexico, nearly everything in our lives was in transition. I focused on my work and the possibilities ahead of me, but the move was much more difficult for my wife and kids.

What helped my wife through all of the changes was Allie, a happy dog that loved everyone but was seldom away from her master. Dogs are known for their faithfulness and the comfort they bring, and she didn't disappoint. Wherever my wife went, so did Allie. She would even take her to work from time to time.

Three years after we moved, Allie died suddenly. It was a terrible day! I could tell that something was wrong. Allie was lying on her side, and Kathy picked her up and held her. You could see in her eyes that the time was near. She never moved during that last hour, and then she took her final breath. We had a short burial for Allie and my wife's heart was broken.

I felt so bad and wanted to help her feel better. Over the next few days, I searched to find another dog like her Allie. In New Mexico, the dog of choice commonly seen is the Chihuahua, which seem to be everywhere. Allie was a Havanese, a small dog weighing around ten pounds, with silky soft hair that doesn't shed. Finding another would not prove to be easy, but my perseverance finally paid off when I found a man who lived close by who was selling two of them. I drove to his house after work, and as I entered his home, I saw five or six dogs running around.

As we talked about the dogs, he shared that he and his ex-wife had been breeders in the past, and the time had come for him to find a good home for a couple of the dogs. I noticed right away that the two he was planning to sell were very timid. When I tried to pet them or pick them up, they would run away and hide. After about twenty minutes, I finally caught one of them and held him on my lap. I instantly could feel the dog shake and want to escape from me. I felt the dog had been neglected and/or abused.

As I was petting the little black and white dog, I knew that he was the one I needed to rescue and take home to Kathy. His life had been a life full of pain and absent of love. He didn't know any other way but cowering in fear. When I brought him home to my wife, he ran away and hid behind our furniture. In the weeks and months ahead, we faced a slow process of helping him learn how to trust us. We decided to name him Bandit because of his coloring and the fact that he was a bit rebellious.

I share this story in conclusion because many of us are exactly like Bandit. We have lived for years in brokenness and pain, wondering if we could ever be free. Our struggles or addictions have become a part of who we are. When I decided to write this book, my goal was to help people find hope by finding freedom. All that I shared within these pages will take intentionality and time. Giving up and going back to where we have been and what we have done before can be so easy. Bandit would have moments where he would let us pet him without running away, but we could see in his eyes that he was still unsure of us.

You will also have times when you may feel unsure, but please know that making these choices and taking these actions are worth it because you are worth it. What you are facing in your life didn't just occur one day; it happened over time. Experiencing freedom doesn't materialize overnight, it will take time and commitment.

You may wonder, *how can I know for sure?* I have seen these principles work in so many people through the years. The good news is that we do not have to walk alone through this journey. First of all, we have God walking alongside of us, giving us strength and support. Secondly, we can reach out to others and build positive friendships. True Freedom comes when we choose to make each of the five choices along with each of the actions found in this book. May you find freedom.

Freedom is realizing, you have a choice.
– T. F. Hodge

"So if the Son sets you free, you are truly free."
– John 8:36

ABOUT THE AUTHOR

 Rick Bosch is originally from the Pacific Northwest but now lives in Albuquerque New Mexico with his wife Kathy. He is a father of five and loves golf, biking and the outdoors. Over the last 16 years he has been a pastor helping people with destructive behaviors and pain. Using his own struggles and experiences, he has developed a practical process to help people find true freedom and hope